A Kindly Scrutiny
of Human Nature

A Kindly Scrutiny
of Human Nature

Essays in Honour of Richard Slobodin

Richard J. Preston, editor

Wilfrid Laurier University Press
[WLU]

We acknowledge the financial support of the Government of Canada through the Book Publishing Industry Development Program for our publishing activities.

Library and Archives Canada Cataloguing in Publication

A kindly scrutiny of human nature : essays in honour of Richard Slobodin / Richard J. Preston, editor.

Includes bibliographical references and index.
Also issued in electronic format.
ISBN 978-1-55458-040-8

1. Slobodin, Richard, 1915–2005.   2. Ethnology—Canada, Northern.
3. Anthropologists—Canada—Biography.   I. Preston, Richard J. (Richard Joseph),
1931–   II. Slobodin, Richard, 1915–2005.

GN29.K46 2009   301   C2008-907619-2

Library and Archives Canada Cataloguing in Publication

A kindly scrutiny of human nature [electronic resource] : essays in honour of Richard Slobodin / Richard J. Preston, editor.

Includes bibliographical references and index.
ISBN 978-1-55458-120-7
Electronic edited collection in PDF, ePub, and XML formats.
Issued also in print format.

1. Slobodin, Richard, 1915–2005.   2. Ethnology—Canada, Northern.
3. Anthropologists—Canada—Biography.   I. Preston, Richard J. (Richard Joseph),
1931–   II. Slobodin, Richard, 1915–2005.

GN29.K46 2009   301

CONTENTS

A Kindly Scrutiny of Human Nature

Richard J. Preston and Harvey A. Feit

Dick Slobodin is for many of us an exemplar of a period in anthropology when the ethnographer's personal qualities established the guidelines for what we now discuss under the rubric of methodology, and when personal perspectives on peoples' actions and intentions directed the selection and balance of more abstract theoretical orientations than are expressed in the written ethnography. Dick knew social and cultural theories with great breadth and depth; he taught the honours theory course for many years and understood the material well enough to avoid selecting any one perspective to guide his thinking and writing.

I chose the title *A Kindly Scrutiny of Human Nature* because it seemed to me that it represented Dick as the person I knew and admired.

Kindly does not mean naive but rather it suggests an undercurrent of humane interest in intentions, actions, and their consequences—and a respect for the simple fact that life looks different to different individuals, even among members of a personal community or intimates in the same family. Dick's respect could and often did show itself in forthright criticism of behaviour that he found lacking in personal decency or social justice, and his files contain a large number of copies of personal letters he sent regarding social justice. *Kindly* has this larger dimension.

Scrutiny is a penetrating gaze that goes far deeper than casual interest. Scrutiny is not the clinical gaze of a French critic's judgment but a clear view of deeper motives and exogenous influences. Dick's personal qualities led him to study people in their whole social and cultural context, first the Gwich'in, then the Metis in the same area—the northern Yukon and northeastern Alaska—and the non-natives there, and the relations between individuals of these groups. Later he turned his gaze inward in order to study a psychiatric anthropologist whose views and personality interested him. And while he had limited opportunity to speak with women, the gender aspect of Gwich'in culture is also served in giving women's views on men's actions and vice versa.

Dick Slobodin anticipated many trends in anthropological thinking. He was reflexive before the term gained currency, he was gender-sensitive without discussing its importance, he paid close attention to nuances of narratives and actions, and so on. He was politically correct because of who he was, not because of critical intellectual currents.

The chapters that follow are the result of a double-session of papers delivered at the annual conference of the Canadian Anthropology Society/ Société Canadienne d'Anthropologie in 2006. The idea for the session came from Doug Hudson, Dick Slobodin's first M.A. student in the early 1970s. Doug volunteered to give a paper on Dene social organization if there were to be a session on Dick's work, but, since he chose not to send it on, I regret that we cannot publish it here. Doug's idea was welcome, since three of the present authors (Damas, Ajzenstat, and myself) had written eulogies about Dick for presentation at his memorial service, and a conference session was the next logical step in honouring Dick's career and expressing something of our memories of him. The double-session jelled nicely, and we agreed to take it the next step, to a Festschrift.

The appropriate starting point for this memorial volume is a brief biography, and since Harvey Feit compiled a fine statement for the university obituary notice soon after Dick's death, it is fitting to use it here, slightly modified. This is followed by the eulogy that I gave at his memorial service. That service, I might add, was conducted by two Anglican priests, Holly Ratcliffe and Paddy Doran, who were anthropology students and friends of Dick's (and also of mine) before they moved on to their religious vocation. It is worth noting that in his later years Dick attended Anglican services and took an active role in them.

Obituary, Professor Richard Slobodin, 1915–2005
Harvey A. Feit

Richard Slobodin, one of the finest ethnographers to work among the First Nations peoples of the Canadian north, and one of the founders of the Department of Anthropology at McMaster University, passed away in

Hamilton, Ontario, on January 22, 2005. Born in New York City on March 6, 1915, he was just short of his ninetieth birthday. Professor Slobodin attended the City College of New York, where he completed a B.A. in comparative literature in 1936 and an M.S. in education in 1938. During and after his studies he worked as a teacher, mainly of English, in New York City high schools.

After completing his master's degree he took a break from teaching and made a career-altering trip to the Yukon Territory in Canada, adjacent to Alaska, where he travelled and did research among the Gwich'in people of the Fort McPherson region through the winter from September 1938 to May 1939. The trip and his decision afterwards to turn to a career in anthropology probably flowed from his early upbringing. He wrote of his career, "My best preparation consisted of belonging to a family wherein both parents and many associates had broad humanist interests, which led to an early exposure to the literature, folklore, and art of many cultures. I was also fortunate enough to have some excellent teachers.... These influences were much more important than formal majors and minors."

After returning to New York he registered in the Ph.D. program at Columbia University in 1940 and began his career as an anthropologist. But his career was interrupted more than once, and it took a quarter-century before he had a continuing academic position. In 1942 he entered the military and served until 1946. After the war he returned to Columbia to complete his Ph.D. For his doctoral research, which he undertook between August 1946 and May 1947, he returned to the Fort McPherson region with support from the Social Science Research Council and a research fellowship from the Arctic Institute of North America. His return to the Gwich'in was a mutually happy one. Dick commented that as a returning visitor he was not treated as "a formidable official sort of person." And he reported that Chief Julius remarked of him on one festive occasion that he was the fellow whom the people had previously "taken in when he was just a poor boy" (Slobodin, 1969: 57).

Following his doctoral field research, he began his university teaching career with assistant professor appointments at the University of Southern California (1947–49) and Los Angeles State College (1950–51). But in 1951 the latter institution notified him that he was not eligible for reappointment. His career was interrupted by his being named in the U.S. congressional investigation into "un-American activities" headed by Senator Joseph McCarthy. Dick, along with many other anthropologists and academics, had been monitored by the FBI and other agencies through the 1940s, presumably because he was thought to have associated with socialist or communist organizations.[1] The McCarthy hearings used innuendo, guilt by association, and testimony offered under threat to besmirch the reputations of many academics and intellectuals as security risks. The hearings also succeeded in barring many from academic employment in the early Cold War era in the United States.

Dick seldom spoke of the 1951–58 period in later years, but in one of his curriculum vitae he described his activities during that time with poignancy—and without bitterness—as "jobs outside anthropology, mostly in California and Mexico." For part of the period (1954–58) he worked with several social work agencies in California. In the decade following 1948 his first three children were born.

In 1959 Dick was able to complete his doctoral dissertation and his degree, and he started to get employment in anthropology. In 1959–60 he was a research associate at Cornell University. The following year he took part in a child-rearing study in Washington, D.C., and in 1960 he was hired for two years as a lecturer at Smith College in Northampton, Massachusetts. He moved to Canada in 1962 for an eighteen-month contract as a senior research officer with the research centre in the Department of Northern Affairs and National Resources. During his time in Ottawa he also took contracts with the National Museum of Canada, but it was made clear by immigration officials that he was not to be given any work related to national security.

The positions in Ottawa afforded him the opportunity to continue doing the research he obviously loved in the North. He had returned to visit peoples in communities in the Yukon in 1961, with a grant from the U.S. National Science Foundation, and in 1962 did research among the Gwich'in of Arctic Red River with support from the National Museum of Canada. His first monograph on the Gwich'in appeared in 1962, *Band Organization of the Peel River Kutchin* (National Museum of Canada). In 1963 he did a groundbreaking social and economic survey of Metis in the Mackenzie District of the Northwest Territories, which provided the basis for his second book, *Metis of the Mackenzie District* (Canadian Research Centre for Anthropology, 1966). He returned to northwestern Canada and adjacent parts of Alaska in 1966 (for the National Museum of Canada), 1968 (with a Canada Council research grant), and 1977 (as an associate of the Northern Yukon Research Program, University of Toronto). During these periods he spoke Gwich'in "with fair fluency," and although he was hoping to improve his competency, he noted that he was one of only three researchers "with any appreciable knowledge of the language," the other two being linguists. (He knew French, Russian, and German as well.)

When McMaster University sought to introduce an anthropology program Dick was highly recommended by his colleagues and McMaster invited him to take up an appointment as associate professor in the Department of Sociology and Anthropology, with a mandate to develop the program. At the time of his initial appointment to McMaster, in 1964, the question of his receiving permanent residency status in Canada had become an issue with the government. It was an odd question, for he had already spent nearly five years in Canada including his northern research trips. His application received support from the university and the faculty association, and after some worrisome delays Dick became a permanent resident of Canada in 1964. He was granted citizenship in his adopted country in 1970.

Thus he was fifty years old when he found an academic "home." He immediately set out to build the anthropology program and to hire colleagues. But he also worked to make it feel like a home to others who would join him. Dick Slobodin had a profound influence on the character, not just the development, of first the program and then the Department of Anthropology. He exemplified a graceful scholarly collegiality. He welcomed and encouraged thoughtful repartee, and his example of engaging in a common endeavour encouraged others to respond in kind. He carefully cultivated relationships with colleagues, students, and friends, and many who knew him throughout academia treasured their relationships with him.

Although he was a specialist on the Canadian North, he did not offer a course in the subject until 1969 because, as he put it, he "put [his] own predilections and interests aside in favour of developing the anthropology program at McMaster." Dick was in effect the associate chairman for anthropology of the Department of Sociology and Anthropology during the formative years 1964–1971, although he served de facto and without formal title until the last two of those years.

His leadership by example and his subtle mentoring continued after he was promoted to professor in 1969, after anthropology became a separate department in 1973, and even after his retirement in 1981. His was an active retirement. He continued to teach courses for many years, to participate in department events, and to undertake entirely new research and publications.

When he took ill early in 2005 and was in hospital, it turned out that he was being cared for by nursing staff and visited by clergy, a number of whom had taken his courses and who spoke both of their admiration for Dick as a teacher and in some cases of the influence he had on their lives.

The lives of many of his colleagues and students were enriched by his presence.

His courses were always thoroughly engaging, communicating his constant intellectual inquisitiveness, his exceptionally diverse knowledge, his passion for learning and teaching, and his profound respect for students. He nurtured and encouraged their intellectual and personal growth with an unpretentious but rare combination of entertaining stories, a sympathetic and judiciously critical sense of human character and foibles, a quiet but pervasive sense of humour, thought-provoking generalizations, and a commitment to standards without being rigidly judgmental. His classes and his person were memorable.

Dick's academic interests extended to aspects of the history of anthropology and related disciplines in addition to his over fifty years of research and publications on the ethnography and ethnohistory of subarctic First Nations. His monographs on the Gwich'in and on the Metis were analytical ethnographies of little-studied places and peoples that revealed their diversity and often unexpected complexity. In 1978 he published what has since become the standard biography of W.H.R. Rivers (New York: Columbia University Press; reprinted 1997), a little-studied key figure in early-twentieth-century anthropology, psychology, and psychiatry, who contributed to field research methods, the study of kinship, and the first recognition and treatment of shell-shock victims during World War I.

Dick's book on Rivers was an inspiration to others beyond academia. The novelist Pat Barker wrote a celebrated trilogy set around World War I, the first volume of which, *Regeneration*, was made into a film and the third of which, *The Ghost Road*, won the Booker Prize. The novels focus in part on an imagined relationship between Rivers and his patient Siegfried Sassoon, the renowned English poet. The books are an extraordinarily rich and challenging examination of manliness, war, pacifism, trauma, and recovery. Asked how she found out about Rivers and started to develop the idea of the first novel, Barker replied, "There's a very short biography by somebody called Richard Slobodin. Rivers was a very secretive man, immensely so. And even when he wasn't being secretive, his handwriting was illegible—"

Interviewer: Ideal for a fiction writer, his illegibility?
Barker: Yes, and a nightmare for a biographer.[2]

After his retirement Dick co-edited a book with Antonia Mills, *Amerindian Rebirth: Reincarnation Belief among North American Indians and Inuit* (Toronto: University of Toronto Press, 1994). This volume—a widely cited work in anthropology and religious studies—explores its subject with the finesse required to respect indigenous peoples and to avoid comfortable but reductionist explanations.

In addition Dick published numerous academic papers on topics as diverse as those of his books. He had an eye for situations and topics that seemed marginal and overlooked, and a knack for revealing their importance. This is clear in his early decision to do research on Metis and in papers he did—for example, on an escaped American slave who was a near mythic figure in the late-nineteenth-century Northwest Territories and Yukon and on early indigenous people's involvement with the Klondike gold rush and how that experience ended up supporting rather than undermining "traditions" among Peel River Gwich'in. His keen eye for the unexpected and his ability to humanize people, partly through keen character sketches, led him to unconventional analyses. He wrote on indigenous peoples as agents and not just products of change (1964), and he studied band society warfare, survival, and vengeance with clarity but not sensationalism ("Without Fire," 1975). His recurrent attention to situations at the boundaries of cultures and categories, and to topics that could be considered difficult, gives much of his work a contemporary quality.

His scholarship was characterized throughout by a wide-ranging knowledge of the literature from the classics to the most recent debates, by meticulous consideration of field and archival sources, by his sophisticated analyses, and by his capacity to draw conclusions that mattered.

During his career, Dick received recognition by accepting invitations to be a summer lecturer at Carleton University (1964) and at Dartmouth College (1967), a research associate at Cambridge University's Scott Polar Research Institute (1972–73), and a Snider Bequest Lecturer at the University of Toronto (1975–76). He was a secretary of the Northeastern Anthropological Association (1972–73), a fellow of the American Anthropological Association and of the Royal Anthropological Institute of Great Britain and Ireland, a member of the Canadian Anthropology Society, and a charter associate of the Arctic Institute of North America.

Dick is survived by his wife, Eleanor Warren (Miller), of Dundas, and by seven children: Jennifer Slobodin, Katherine Slobodin McCulloch, and John Slobodin, all of California, and Lisa Miller Kjellberg of Sweden, Roderick Miller of Geneva, Rebecca Miller (Smith) of Ontario, and Peter Miller of Quebec.

EULOGY FOR DICK SLOBODIN

Richard J. Preston, April 2005

One of my responsibilities in eulogizing Dick Slobodin is to ensure that the statements I make do not praise him to the point of making him unrecognizable to those who were privileged to know him. He was sensitive to this problem when, while in hospital, he told Eleanor that if we had a memorial ceremony, someone should report that he failed kindergarten, because the teacher was not too impressed with his maturity. This is *really* vintage Dick, setting our stage and his academic career with humour and humility. Dick was thinking ahead, lest we try to elevate him into a patron sainthood. I'll risk extending his point, suggesting that failing kindergarten may have had to do with a memory problem he once told me about—that he had always had poor short-term memory but excellent long-term memory, and this had been a serious problem for him until he got old enough to have his long-term memory kick in.

He wasn't joking about his long-term memory. For example, Dick's historical grasp of anthropology was simply stunning. In the early 1970s Dick and I split the six-unit History of Anthropological Theory honours seminar. During the fall term, he covered two millennia of social thought, from the pre-Socratics through the nineteenth century. Then, in the winter term, I picked up the chronology "on or about Boas" and covered maybe a half century. For a smooth transition, I accompanied him through his last session in the fall term and realized that he knew so much more than I did that I felt quite dismayed by my inadequacy. My mind went numb, self-protectively, and I had trouble keeping focused for the full three hours. The students, on the other hand—including Jennifer, one of my daughters—because they had no such hard act to follow, simply found him wonderfully well informed.

In 1987 Rula Geyer, then Rula Logotheti, an undergraduate anthropology major, interviewed Dick several times for some autobiographical reminiscences. I want to thank Rula for doing this and for sharing with me now. Dick suggested at that time that the major periods of his life were these:

1. childhood and youth: the first thirty years, 1915–45, ending with the death of his first wife
2. stress and instability: the next twenty-five years, 1945–69
3. stability as a tenured professor and happiness in his marriage to Eleanor: the next thirty-five years

Dick's period of childhood and youth was intellectually and athletically encouraging. He grew up in a socialist family, attended the progressive Ethical Culture School and then university for his B.A. The pivotal experience of his career came in 1938–39, when he travelled by canoe and railway boxcar to the Northwest Territories, wintered on snowshoes with Gwich'in hunters, and then hiked to Alaska. During World War II he travelled some more, this time by aircraft carrier and Grumman F4F Wildcat, before shifting into intelligence work. At the end of his period of childhood and youth came his discovery and acceptance of the fact that Doris Lambert, the woman he loved and wanted to marry, was terminally ill with cancer. They married anyway, and she survived just nine months.

Dick returned for another year (1946–47) with the Gwich'in people, gathering the basis of his Ph.D. dissertation, and on his return he and Jane Smith were married. Jennifer and Katherine were born in the next few years. The McCarthy witch-hunt cost him his teaching job, and personal differences led to divorce. Two years later he married his third wife, June Cannan, and John was born. This marriage lasted fifteen years, until June also was taken by cancer. Dick listed over twenty different jobs in this twenty-five-year period.

The period of stress and turmoil was characterized by his adapting to repeated experiences of separation and loss and sometimes expulsion and contempt from academic and other sources. Perhaps that strengthened his tendency to be unimpressed with regulations. He chose to help the underprivileged rather than hold to organizational requirements—the bureaucratic rules and deadlines that tacitly slighted the personal side of life. I felt mindful of Dick's sensitivity to being slighted, a quality he shared with subarctic hunters. He did not ask us for much beyond common decency, but that decency was very important.

My enduring impression of Dick was first formed when I listened to him read his paper on Gwich'in reincarnation (1970) at the Learneds in 1969, and I will never forget the sensitive humanity he expressed in an unwritten postscript to the paper. Perhaps thirty years after the fieldwork, he contacted a Gwich'in woman who had moved to a city, and visited her for a cup of tea and conversation. Dick related to us that he had known her as a beautiful child of eight and that the intervening years had not been kind to her. When he mentioned the story of her reincarnation she replied, "You remember that, eh? Well, never again, thank you."

We are thankful that Dick's last thirty-five years—when he was husband to Eleanor, stepfather to her four children, and father to his three—*were* kind to him, and we are thankful too that his rare blend of humility, humour, and pride set us an example to emulate. Once again, thanks, Dick. May we all age so well.

NOTES

Richard Preston gratefully acknowledges McMaster University for generously providing a subsidy toward the publication of this volume.

1 For information on the period and a passing reference to Dick, see David H. Price, *Threatening Anthropology* (Durham, NC: Duke University Press, 2004).
2 Interview by Rob Nixon, Rachel Carson Professor of English at the University of Wisconsin–Madison, http://muse.jhe.edu/demo/contemporary_literature/vo45/45.1nixon.html. Unsolicited praise and appreciation for Dick's book, albeit in an offhand sort of way.

CHAPTER ONE

Richard Slobodin's Ethnography and Human Nature

Richard J. Preston

Notions or conceptions of human nature and human identity can be usefully explored by discerning their use in the ethnographic process. Dick Slobodin's ethnography provides a humanist perspective that I explore here. While he did not (to my knowledge) write definitionally about human nature and human identity, his take on the topic comes across with memorable, exemplary effect. Dick did not write a lot, but he wrote very well, in accessible and personable prose.

In the year following the completion of his dissertation, he published two articles, one on anxiety and the second on warfare. The first, "Some Social Functions of Kutchin Anxiety" (1960), contrasts with the then-contemporary studies of subarctic anxiety as socially negative. He summarizes and discusses several cases that show the risks and necessities of trying to keep a personal community together both socially and physically. Becoming lost, or being a solitary survivor, is regarded anxiously as dangerous and unnatural because the condition puts a person's human nature (he uses this term) itself into question. Such persons must be urgently searched for, but if found must be approached with caution, so that they will not bolt back into the bush. A single member of the search party will come forward gradually, kindly, and gently in the hope that the lost person will choose to come back to his human nature. That he is potentially so wild as to be dangerous means that, where kindness fails, he may as a last resort be killed. In some myths, extraordinary solitary persons may re-enter their community only through an ordeal.

The second 1960 paper, on Eastern Kutchin warfare, brings the topic of war down from an organized system emphasizing heroic victory to more spontaneous raiding parties in which planning and discipline are unpredictable and victory is a revenge killing of one or a few people. This paper is in a sense an extension of the previous one, moving beyond lost persons and losing humanity to encountering enemies. Dick is asking us why they are regarded and treated as enemies, and finds a subtle answer. Unlike that of the more westerly Kutchin, Eastern Kutchin warfare is not institutionalized and the raiding is with only one adjacent group—the Eskimo. The Eskimo are the only group for whom the Kutchin have the advantage of being the conveyors of indirect trade in Russian and then Hudson's Bay Company goods. With the establishment of Fort McPherson, the HBCo post at Peel River, this advantage was lost and the raiding stopped. In one potential flare-up some years later, it was the respective Kutchin and Eskimo trading partners, not the HBCo trader or missionaries, that brokered the settlement. They were enemies no longer.

Dick's approach is clear in his care to record what people intended with their words, and to present these intentions with more than respect—with good grace. His prose invites us to participate vicariously in the events and attitudes. His success in this presentation is due to his presenting people without objectification or other reduction. Rather than show only those facets of his subjects' behaviour that illustrate service to some abstract point, he gives us a picture of persons identifiable to us as fellow humans. Perhaps it is fair to say that he shows integrity without pride or idealizing, and with an underlying good humour that might be his own or might be that of the persons doing the talking—or both.

"The Dawson Boys" (1963) takes up relations between a sizeable number of the Peel River Kutchin (men) and white men—specifically the gold seekers—and again finds the Kutchin demonstrating moderation and adaptability, experimenting and adventuring without becoming dependent or demoralized, making money by selling meat and by working the boats, and retaining good memories.

"The Subarctic Metis as Products and Agents of Culture Contact" (1964) is a short preview of his 1966 book, and together preview and book complete Slobodin's sociological mosaic of the Mackenzie region. The 1964 paper in brief and general terms describes Metis as a distinctive adaptation to the fur trade—the men voyaging or transporting in summer and hunting and trapping in winter, while women and children were more associated with a particular trading post. A comparison to the temporary adaptation of the Kutchin men who became known as the Dawson Boys would have been in Dick's mind, but he does not speak of it.

"Leadership and Participation in a Kutchin Trapping Party" (1969) is an extension of materials in his dissertation, and Dick framed the paper within the scholarly literature of comparative small-scale social organization in order to speak to the conference on band societies. For all its scholarly referencing, it contains the specifics of person and place in its account of a marten-trapping expedition into the Richardson Mountains. The examination of the use and meanings of kin terms is now dated, yet the issue is that of identity—of self in relation to others. And his discussion of kinship identity and relations describes the personal qualities of leadership and followership that the trapping expedition embodied. For these same conference proceedings Dick provides introductory remarks and points of discussion on criteria for the identification of bands" (1969)—another level of identity.

In a textbook chapter, "The Indians of Canada Today: Questions on Identity" (1972), he goes beyond band societies and reviews the history and variety of types of groups of North American indigenous peoples in order to set the stage for the hypothetical question of what a contemporary and comprehensive picture of Indian groups, both land-based people and urbanizing people, might be expected to show if an updated study were done.

"The Chief Is a Man" (1971) is a brief explanation and corrective regarding the visage of a famous Kutchin chief of the late nineteenth century, when chiefs were young men who made impressive efforts to appear fashionably wealthy. The photo of the subject of the original drawing had been mis-perceived as female. See his paper on Alexander Hunter Murray (1981).

"The Metis of Northern Canada" (1972) is a brief summary of his 1968 book on the social and cultural characteristics of the Northern Metis of the Mackenzie Valley and on points of comparison between that group and the Red River Metis. With words well chosen, and from the underlying perspective of a shared humanity that binds Metis, Indian, Eskimo, and white, he constructs from their social categories and value statements a feel for the Metis as a cultural adaptation to the fur trade frontier.

In "Canadian Subarctic Athapaskans in the Literature to 1965" (1975), Slobodin completes his survey of people involved in the region. Having first written of Kutchin men and women, both from the remembered past and as observed in his ethnographic present, he then drew on stories of Eskimo men and women, and then on the fur trade phenomenon of Metis families. In this paper he goes further to include the explorers, traders, missionaries, and travellers-sportsmen, followed by twentieth-century ethnographers, including himself. Ethnohistorians get their place in "Some Recent Developments in Subarctic Culture History and Ethnohistory: Comments" (1980), where he opens up intellectually critical views such as:

1. the differences between ideology and action
2. the linkages of power, control, and gender
3. distinctions between cultural stability and ephemera
4. the varieties of reflexivity among observers
5. the challenge of accounting for human misery and creativity

"Without Fire: A Kutchin Tale of Warfare, Survival, and Vengeance" (1975) is an example I find especially good for validating my claim, partly because it is a tale and therefore close to my own area of interpretive experience, and partly because a good story has an aesthetic integrity that highlights the morality underlying it. The plot is of a warrior who escapes an attack on his band, survives a harsh winter without fire to keep himself from freezing or to cook his food with, and who, after a year, manages to wreak vengeance on his enemies. There are comments on the story by other folks in the area and agreement by the storyteller to their additions. Relevant abstract comments by scholars are footnoted. But there is more, and a fuller aesthetic balance.

The epic warrior story of triumph over terrible adversity is impressive. And of course it is very masculine. As it happens, the story tells us that this man had a wife of uncommon cleverness, skills, and beauty—what was called a prize woman. Traditionally a prize woman was the object of raiding; she was liable to be kidnapped and forced into becoming a trophy wife for the raiding party's leading warrior. In this story, the woman's words and point of view are treated with care and humanity, and the woman herself is given the last word. In her later years and faced yet again with a raid to kidnap her, she says she is now old, with children and grandchildren all over the region. She says her fire burns low, and she refuses to move again. Then, with a tone of finality, she says these men are acting like little boys. Her final words are deeply humorous—deeper than the fighting passion of men and the serial polyandrous career of an extraordinary woman. The drama has reached the place where it is time to end the killing, end the seizing of a prize woman as a trophy of powerful warriors, and realize how it all looks from the vantage point of an elder's wisdom.

In "Kutchin Concepts of Reincarnation" (1970), the humanist pattern appears again, in the kindness Dick shows as he describes the beliefs using ethnographic examples, and in the kindness he shows in the postscript, in which he recounts the conversation he had with the Kutchin woman who, when told she had been reincarnated, responded, "Well, never again, thank you." Her quiet decisiveness speaks to us all in its eloquently understated assessment of the harsh life she had experienced. Like the old woman who characterizes the warriors and her own desirability as a woman as nothing but passionate foolishness, Dick is trying to penetrate into our human nature with a kindly and rather sad gaze. The result is that an intimacy is established between us and the personal identity he describes, an intimacy that touches our common humanity. He does this so tenderly that it would likely be embarrassing to the persons he portrays, to be so revealed to an audience of their friends, much less an audience located behind the mask of the printed page. But I want to point out that he treats himself and his own experiences in the same way, as in an unpublished essay from 1938 in which he describes a hunt he participated in. It was rejected for publication, but this one deserves another chance, and so it is included as the closing chapter in this volume.

This exposure to scrutiny, and the attendant risk of embarrassment, was made clear in an unpublished paper from 1988. In it, Dick tells of a middle-aged woman he spoke with who had become a well-known politician and who was one of the children of an Inuit named Elsie. Elsie was a girl of sixteen when, one night in the 1920s, she sought refuge from an abusive stepfather and ran to the cabin of two white trappers. They assured her that they would not bother her, and, after staying for a while with these men, she married one of them—Reidar, a Scandanavian trapper.

One story in particular seems to have engaged his imagination in a way that seems to me to be the culmination of his concern to portray all the people of the Lower Mackenzie Valley in their common humanity. It's the story of Black Tom, the Christlike fugitive slave who arrives in the valley, sojourns for some time, lives a gentle and exemplary life there, and then disappears. Again Slobodin's characteristic gaze is evident—not a clinical gaze but one of empathy and kindness sometimes touched with gentle humour or deep sadness. In some moments, as in the story of Black Tom, I sense something of the trickster behind Dick's gaze, and perhaps in the Kutchin storytellers themselves—the absurd warrior and beautiful woman, the damaged soul of the urban native woman reincarnated only to suffer the indignities of a marginal life in the city, the engineered wedding of an Eskimo girl to a Scandanavian trapper, and finally Black Tom, the heroic escaped slave whose memory was revered by the Kutchin but who was forgotten by the aristocratic explorer who befriended him. I think that for Dick, the goal of ethnography within humanist scholarship is more personal than Geertz's "enlarging the universe of human discourse" (*The Interpretation of Cultures*, 1973) in his searching to discern, understand, and appreciate humble and profound truths about us all.

Dick researched and wrote his book on W.H.R. Rivers during the 1970s, when he was happily married and his academic life was relatively stable and rewarding. In this study he brings us full circle. *W.H.R. Rivers* is an ethnography of a person—not of Dick himself, but close enough. It's of a professional with very broad interests, an M.D. who became an experimental psychologist, a psychotherapist, a psychiatrist, a social anthropologist. The book is a presentation of Rivers' life in three parts of roughly equal length, a biography, the salient intellectual themes in his career, and selections from Rivers' writings. This combination seems to shadow Slobodin's ethnographic writing, with portions of individuals' lives, salient cultural themes, and verbatim narratives.

I do not know why Dick chose to study Rivers (1864–1922) but suspect he was drawn to one of the seminal psychological and social thinkers of the early twentieth century partly because he appreciated Rivers' ability to support unpopular perspectives, to do several kinds of outstanding and collaborative laboratory and field research, and, without embarrassment, to change his mind in response to his research findings. During the First World War, Rivers left Cambridge to work compassionately and therapeutically with shell-shock victims, some of whom became enduring friends. All his adult life he engaged in enthusiastic and encouraging discussions with students, patients, and junior colleagues, treating them as if they were his peers. He became widely celebrated and honoured professionally. And in his final year, he abandoned his conservative political detachment to becoming an active Labour Party candidate.

In other words, Rivers was an excellent and influential scholar and a decent person. I believe that Slobodin regretted the too-facile and dismissive judgment passed on professionals in the human sciences at the turn of the twentieth century by the late-twentieth-century intellectuals who were Dick's peers and students. Perhaps he saw in Rivers an under-appreciated person who was in this regard comparable to an escaped American slave, an abused Inuit girl, Gwich'in peoples, Metis peoples, and others. I believe he saw himself as closer in his sentiments to these marginalized folks than to many of his own colleagues. On the first page of the Rivers book, Dick writes:

Yet one must sympathize with critics of Rivers, for theirs is a tricky under-taking. Finding fault with some of Rivers' hypotheses is like shooting fish in a barrel. But this fish is a slippery one; while critics are happily pursu-ing their sport, Rivers is off doing something else that, on balance, leaves them at times looking rather foolish. (Slobodin 1978: vii)

Critics may easily find fault with his early evolutionism, or his later diffu-sionism, or his support of Freudian analysis, and so on ... but when you shoot fish in a barrel, what happens to the barrel? Or to your face? Trick-ster lives on.

FROM BRIAN CRAIK, GRAND COUNCIL OF THE CREES
AND A FORMER STUDENT IN THE DEPARTMENT

Thanks for sending the news on Dick Slobodin. He attracted me to anthro-pology with his humble yet proud way of carrying himself and his inter-est in others. I am very sorry to hear that he is ill and confined to the hospital. I remember his sense of humour, his humanity, and his friendship, and will always carry this with me as I am sure many others will. I will always be grateful to his support and kindness and glad that I was able to get to know him.

FROM GARY KOFINAS, UNIVERSITY OF ALASKA,
FAIRBANKS

Dick came to Gwich'in country many years ago as a young man, and did an early canoe trip down the Mackenzie, up the Rat, and then on the Por-cupine before the Second World War.... Taken with his experience, he later returned to do fieldwork for his Ph.D. dissertation with the people of Fort McPherson and wrote several wonderful papers on the Peel River Indians (as they were called at that time) and on the Gwich'in people of Alaska and Canada. Dick's understanding of and relationship with the people was unusual and his writing is best described as wonderfully elo-quent. In his writings he referred to the people he worked with as com-munity (not as tribal, like some others did in those times), and he highlighted the Gwich'in relationship with caribou as critical. In the mid-1990s I asked Johnny Charlie Sr. about Dick, and Johnny remembered him with kind words and distinguished him from some less-than-good anthropologists who had worked there. When I visited with Dick years ago at McMaster University, well after he retired, he talked at length about his memorable friends from the Delta....

Much is changing quickly in the northern world that Dick loved, and the inspiration of his work and his ethic will serve us all well into the future.

From John Tetlichi, a Gwich'in leader

As you know when someone that we have connection with, and that has done a lot of work for the Aboriginal community, falls ill we are all saddened. Knowing that he knew my Dad is very touching. In those days these researchers got right down to earth, meaning they ate with us, shared with us, but above all respected how we were trying to keep our culture and tradition strong. I did not know Dick, however I take my hat off to him. I want to thank him for all the good work and memories that he treasures. May the creator look down upon you in time of need.

From Sandi Warren, Metis Ph.D. student, Native Studies, Trent University

Dr. Richard Slobodin passed away early Saturday morning in his 90th year. Dr. Slobodin was an anthropologist and professor emeritus at McMaster University.

For many who studied with Dr. Slobodin or read his research, such as [his writing on the] Metis of the Mackenzie District, he may be regarded as one of many "white" anthropologists who "studied" Aboriginal people. However, please allow me to introduce to you the Dr. Slobodin that I know. Colleagues speak of Dr. Slobodin as gentle, courtly mannered, and vastly knowledgeable in literature and history. What people might not know is how his work was inspired by the people he encountered along his journey.

His interest and much of his work was inspired by a visit in 1938 to territories of the north Aboriginal communities of the Mackenzie district, where he shares that through the generosity of the Northern peoples: he became aware of a knowledge and way of life that was sophisticated, ecologically astute, and quite different from life in the south. Dr. Slobodin shares that the experience deeply impacted him, who as "a young, vigorous, and perhaps used to the 'mainstream' way of thinking, he journeyed to the North but returned, deeply inspired by values of responsibility, respect and reciprocity."

As a Metis person, I was fortunate to have known Dr. Slobodin. He shared with me his personal journey, insights, and love. He would pass along

texts and readings that I would pore over to feed my own personal journey toward understanding colonialism, history, and the Metis. Ironically,
today I am able to challenge the readings as an Aboriginal person and
scholar. But I will remain grateful for the push and critical debates that we
engaged in during our time together. You see, as coincidence would have
it, I first met Dr. Slobodin, "Uncle Dick," at a family gathering twenty
years ago. Dr. Slobodin is my husband's uncle. Thus, over the past twenty
years, I was able to know the scholar and the man. I share his passing
today as a way of honouring a scholar who has brought to the academy
Metis people's experience and the person, a member of my family, whom
I respect and love.

FROM PETER STEPHENSON, UNIVERSITY OF VICTORIA

[I just finished reading your obituary for Dick. Thank you for writing such
a beautiful piece, Harvey.] In my five years at McMaster, Dick was someone for whom I—like so many others—developed an enormous respect and
affection. Reading your piece reminded me once again of the many fine
qualities of the man and of the role that a true mentor can play in the
lives of others. I certainly learned some lessons about how to work and live
from Dick, more by example than anything else. There were so many fine
moments—from playing on the department softball team (we were the
only faculty on the team—the youngest and oldest people in the department), to hilarious ironic asides at department meetings that had gone on
for far too long. He was a presence, even long after I had left the department, and I shall always remember him. Thanks to your obituary, I'll have
an even more vivid memory.

CHAPTER TWO

Dick Slobodin: The Anthropology of a Divided Self

Sam Ajzenstat

Dick Slobodin and I, anthropologist and philosopher, came to McMaster in the same year some forty years ago. I feel privileged to have had him as a friend over those forty years, and I think I came to know a few things about someone who was, after all, a very private man.

Dick's practice of anthropology, which held social embeddedness and detachment together without trying to resolve the tensions in that double vision, was an expression not only of his intellectual convictions but also of the definition of the human that he found in his own temperament. His love of literature and philosophy gave him the concept of anthropology as a challenge to the idea that social life could express all of a person. In his anthropology, as in his life, the responsibilities of community existed side by side with an unsatisfiable, lonely individuality. The combination made him an increasingly rare humanizing force against the terrible simplifiers who see the mandate of the university as ideological social engineering.

Dick in person was such a powerful presence that it is hard to resist treating even some of the small personal details of his life as if they were archetypes. From what I knew of Dick, for example, I have drawn my own explanation of why—as he ruefully but not without a touch of pride told his friends—he failed kindergarten. He was far from being a "failure": it is for us a symbol not only of one of his great virtues but also of the price one has to pay for such virtues. I can't help imagining that whenever the kindergarten teacher made some simple statement, Dick was already then the kind of person who would start to turn it over and over, letting it reveal itself as infinitely many-sided and quivering with uncertainties that required a slow, painstaking teasing out of everything it might or might not contain. I see him staring out the window, stopped dead by each sentence while his less reflective fellow students move on to the next one. I see him at last learning—with a touch of disappointment that he never completely lost—that success at school or anywhere always means leaving behind an infinitely extended trail of unresolved alternatives.

The phrase "unresolved alternatives" summons up another Slobodin idiosyncrasy-turned into-archetype—his resistance to the word processor. A note from Dick was a veritable palimpsest, a layer of old Underwood script covered with cross-outs, scrawled-in rewrites, and rewrites of rewrites—a record of the movement of a living mind and of what it was to be human that, at least in our more romantic moments, we fear the delete button is about to make us forget.

These are pictures that fit together to show us a lot of what made Dick an unforgettable friend and what made him the kind of liberating teacher that the mind can't stay alive without; yet in the modern university, with its problem-solving, world-fixing orientation, this is something that is much less appreciated than it should be.

One of the most influential things—unfortunately—that Karl Marx ever said was that the point of thought was not to understand the world but to change it. But Dick, though certainly a man of the left, was also a man of conservative temperament who believed that understanding *was* the point. Not only did understanding come first, but it would take forever. Any attempt to realize Marx's unity of theory and practice would be a distortion of the divided human self. In the meantime, if intellectual life, and perhaps especially anthropology, had any mandate it was to resist oversimplified solutions and attempts to pin down human nature without ever giving up the idea that there is such a thing. As a reflective person, Dick could see that relativism and absolutism by themselves were equally oversimplifications. They need each other and yet remain irreconcilable. Human beings are a complicated lot. Just when you think you have them pinned down, they surprise you. They cherish their idiosyncrasies, even the less constructive ones. And as an anthropologist, so did Dick. From the ancient Greek tragedies he had learned the unbreakable connection between the best of us and the worst. In consequence, that one might alleviate ills but never eliminate them was at the heart of his moderate activism. So in the classroom Dick was neither a problem-solver nor a world-fixer. When I think of him as a teacher—he occasionally invited me to participate in his classes—I think of Kierkegaard's remark that his job was not to make things easier but to make them harder.

It was all the more extraordinary that Dick had a way of doing this without generating intolerable frustration in his young students. Part of what it required was his knowledge of the ins and outs of the history of anthropological theory. But there was something more.

The idea that the word "anthropology" is pretty much a synonym for the word "humanities" was something that Dick could savour—and not just because of his wide knowledge of languages and his interest in word derivations. His anthropology always led back to the humanities and the humanities always led back to storytelling. As everyone who knew him was aware, Dick was, almost above everything else, a storyteller. These stories were of course often the stories of the native people of the North. But a description Harvey Feit has given of Dick as studying "band society warfare, survival and vengeance with clarity but not sensationalism" is an excellent reminder that Homer's *Iliad*, Virgil's *Aeneid*, and all, even the least well known, of Shakespeare's plays were seldom far from Dick's thoughts. For him, these were places we had to keep going back to in search of ourselves. As he layered one story on top of another, anyone listening to him would get a hint of all the incompatible things that human beings have to try to put together in order to be fully themselves, and the various tragedies and comedies that result. To the right listeners, Dick's effect could be truly shamanistic. This tall, slender man of aristocratic posture and neat white beard, quietly and slowly—always slowly because every detail was essential—leading you through the labyrinth of human decision and action could be profoundly liberating, setting you free from the terrible simplifiers.

None of this is to say that Dick was anything like a wishy-washy person who avoided decisions or commitments. Quite the contrary. The Olympian ability to hear all the stories would, on its own, also be an oversimplification of the human. One also had to live one's own story. Dick saw and tried to teach others how to see with a double vision, something that is well described in a couple of lines in Walt Whitman's "Song of Myself": "Looking with side-curved head curious what will come next / Both in and out of the game and watching and wondering at it." At a time when many find "embeddedness" an attractive and perhaps even complete account of a healthy human existence, Dick found the most fully human in the tension between embeddedness and unimbeddedness.

But to live with the tension between membership and detached understanding, craving full integration and finding it perpetually out of reach, can't be as easy as Whitman often makes it sound. So I want to end by coming back to one last combination of contraries in Dick Slobodin. On the one hand, Dick was, especially in the years of his marriage to Eleanor, a very happy man. He was conspicuously a man who was deeply grateful, indeed who felt blessed by and close to his family and friends, and he was both loving and compassionate in return. He was these things all the more so because of the craving for something that he knew he was not going to get—I've called it understanding, but it might be better called more broadly a complete coming together of the inner and the outer person and one person with another. That sense of an unsatisfiable craving was what made him a great teacher and a great person, demanding the best from others and from himself in a patient and loving way. But the result, on the other hand, even at his happiest and closest to others, was a streak of loneliness, a sadness, usually muted, usually patient, but not always. On occasion he could seem very far away.

Yet he always came back and always with the heartfelt apology of the gentleman he was. It might have been his Jewish background that awakened in him that sense of human exile, which was one of the most powerful things he had to teach. It is that same sense of exile that we hear in Dick's favourite song, that great "hymn" written by the son of a synagogue cantor working with a Jewish socialist, "Somewhere Over the Rainbow," which Dick's daughter Jennie sang at his memorial service at McMaster University. I don't think that Dick could quite believe that there really was a "somewhere over the rainbow." But he understood as deeply as anybody why there ought to be, and why we ought never to forget the other side even while we have to live on this side.

CHAPTER THREE

Slobodin as Example: A Note on a Dialectics of Style

Kenneth Little

It was wickedly hot and humid on a late-August afternoon in 1978 when Dick Slobodin began a story to illustrate a point about a section of my M.A. thesis on Paul Radin and life history as theory and method in anthropology. Nothing bizarre in that, only the conversation took place while we were nervously perched on the roof of his very handsome house. His job was to anchor my legs while I anxiously bent over the roof to paint the house eaves. This was his idea. I can't remember why I agreed to it. And I cannot for the life of me remember the specifics of his story, something to do with Dostoevsky on form and content, but I do remember how I felt while, in the middle of it, he let go of my legs. Dick had become preoccupied with figuring out some historical literary fact and hadn't noticed that I was quickly slipping over the roof. I screamed. He calmly grabbed both the point he was looking for and my legs out of mid air. I somehow scrambled back onto the roof as he finished talking, only to confront his puzzled look. Had I not understood what he was trying to say? Reading my shock and confusion and feeling the heat of the late afternoon, he declared the day's work complete. It was time to wash up and get ready for what had become, over the week I spent painting his house, my favourite time of the day—evening drinks with Dick, his family, and friends.

I remember each evening seemed to conjure a different invited guest or professional acquaintance and new topics of conversation. The conversation was infectious and highly enjoyable. Dick would watch such conversations grow and often nudge them along with stories relying on his unique style of storytelling, in a manner that made us all feel comfortable and valued. I remember wishing that my every summer evening could be spent in such a refined and exciting environment. With a modest, almost shy demeanour that complemented the sense of humour he used both kindly and prudently, Dick could mould his stories around most subjects of conversation or debate to develop a critical and thought-provoking sense of human nature and its quirkiness. He usually had something thoughtful to say and often said it through an example or with a story in mind. His delightful informal style of storytelling counted, just as his more formal advice and reasoned judgment always did.

I remember some of his stories, too, like the one when, while he was still a high-school student, his family, who were committed to issues of social justice and to democratic political change, housed various international leaders of social democratic movements, a veritable who's who of international socialism at the time. Or his first impressions of canoeing into the Canadian North, or the hardships he endured after being blacklisted by McCarthy's House Committee on Un-American Activities. Yet it is his style of storytelling that I remember most, and not just during those memorable evenings on the Slobodins' verandah. It was also during the sometimes intense discussions we had while I was writing my M.A. thesis.

I wish I still had the thirty-some pages of single-spaced notes he made on what I foolishly thought to be the final draft of my thesis on the anthropologist Paul Radin. Each comment was marked by a page, paragraph, and line reference and gestured toward his commitment to uncompromising standards of writing and thinking as well as to his encyclopedic knowledge, not only of the anthropology I was drawing on but also of its place in the history of anthropology and its philosophical underpinnings. It was the detail and patience he brought to thesis editing, from first to last word, that impressed and challenged me. His criticism was rendered out of goodwill, with not a hint of suspicion or of doubt about my ability to do the work. He agreed with little more than my organization of the facts of Radin's life, some of the impact and history of which, as David Price's "Threatening Anthropology: McCarthyism and the FBI's Surveillance of Activist Anthropologists" demonstrates, crossed his own.[1] Slobodin was not ready to endorse my radical hermeneutic approach, but neither was he judgmental. He knew the tradition and encouraged me to rewrite my thesis and argue it out with him, point by point. It was his example of dedication and collegiality, and my impression that our projects were of common purpose—whether we were perched on his roof, relaxing over drinks, or chatting in the department—that made me confident about what I was saying and the significance of saying it.

I know Richard Slobodin more through his wisdom and his example of scholarly life than I do through his writings. So my impression of him is more personal and historical than abstract and textual. To tell you the truth, I haven't read that much of his work other than his 1962 Peel River book and several of his essays on the Gwich'in, including one remarkably brave paper taking anthropologists of the Dene to task for their lack of theoretical perspective, and his 1978 book on W.H.R. Rivers, a copy of which he gave to me with the inscription "To Ken, With best regards. Another part of the history of anthropology that might interest you. Dick Slobodin. Dec. '78." When I think about him now there is a shadow voice reminding me that whatever I might do in anthropology, I could not think theory or write ethnography or life history like he did. Then I hear the disturbing echo: nor, because it was so unusually and beautifully written and so meticulously researched with the discerning care of a exemplary thinker, could I. Envy mixed with dread. A politics and poetics of representation played off against the moral form that his writing took both as structure and content; a productive conflict, never resolved, but one that still returns in my imaginary conversations with him. This is the matter of the historical effect of an enduring style of writing and thinking as it rubs off and plays a part in another's intellectual life as example.

Several years ago Sally Price initiated a project on the history of important figures in Canadian anthropology. Inspired by her initiative I contacted Slobodin, some years retired from his teaching duties at McMaster but no less active—in social justice and writing projects—than he had ever been, and explained that I would like to interview him for her project. My intention was to write a short intellectual and personal life history of Richard Slobodin, in his own words. At first Slobodin politely demurred. But months later I received a short letter from him saying that he had reconsidered the request. Why, I am not sure. But he had worked out how he wanted to structure the interviews and what topics he wanted to cover. We met once to discuss the project.

I still have my notes on that conversation, undated fragments of ideas that set out a rough guideline and various topics. We would range widely, summarizing his intellectual biography, including formative influences and various theoretical preoccupations, his Dene research and the problems and opportunities for future anthropological research in the North, ethics, McMaster anthropology and Canadian anthropology, and his Rivers research, among them. From my notes, however, and it was always my impression, Slobodin was also willing to explore something of his personal life and personal and political influences and engagements, by no means a small or insignificant part of his story. But he wanted the story to be balanced. My notes include a heavily underlined phrase in capital letters—NO ROMANCE/NO NOSTALGIA. Slobodin neither imagined nor intended the project to be a complete account of his life and career. Rather, it was to contain signposts to other narratives, stories, references, and allusions, which he hoped we might explore as stories in their own right. From the start, then, we agreed that there would be multiple principles of narrative order and that stories were central to the project. His "career" was one such principle and he insisted on some loose chronological perspective, but his career as a moral tale was meant to be crosscut with other autobiographical stories, impressions, and stories-within-stories. In addition, there were other topics like "education in anthropology and allied subjects" and "fieldwork in the North," which, though drawing on autobiographical materials, were meant partly as intellectual history, partly as memoir, and partly as theoretical critique.

Sadly, after all the planning, we never followed through on the project. I was chair of my department at the time when our planning met with the historical contingencies of a nasty and long CUPE strike at York. The strike became my sole preoccupation and it took all of my time and energy. Dick understood that. Yet after the strike we were never able to find a suitable time for the two of us to meet and we eventually gave up trying.

I like to think that the conversation we planned would not only have focused on the moral purposes and historical merit of his intellectual work and career but would also have acted as an unrehearsed intellectual adventure, a performative production of an intellectual and personal life history. I think Slobodin's work and life formed a productive dialectic between the formalism of his intellectual work and comportment and his adventurous life as an early-twentieth-century Northern explorer and ethnographer, a lifelong social activist committed to social change, and a storyteller with a shrewd sense of history and culture. In other words, Slobodin was a formal man who interacted with others with a quirky frankness that was polite, reserved, and firm. With the wisdom of manners that I had somehow learned to associate with the elegance, demeanour, and formal conduct of professorial culture but had not—until I met Slobodin—yet experienced, he remained an imposing figure. Yet he seemed able to find the funny side of things, making observations culled from his sustained engagement with the various everyday worlds he inhabited. The human condition provided him with the raw material to exercise that other less formal and more endearing side, one filled with wit and his own style of charm.

It was the complications and tensions of this double-sidedness—a formality without grandness in tension with a personable informality, commanding without being superior—that made Slobodin such a seductive and perplexing scholarly example.

I'll end with this image of Slobodin's double-sidedness as an arresting image, but let me connect it with a final observation that comes in the way of another image. When I look at the picture of W.H.R. Rivers on the cover of Slobodin's book on the man, I see Richard Slobodin. I have conflated the two in an unrealistic, imaginative elision; the image for me works as both copy and contact. In an interview my colleague Naomi Adelson conducted with Slobodin in 1999, which focused on his Rivers work, she asked him why he became interested in Rivers and why he wrote about him. Slobodin answers: "It's a mystery to me.... I don't know what impelled me to come up with Rivers. But I always thought, as I hoped many other people would, I thought he was an interesting anthropologist" (Adelson, 2001: 8).

To me it's not such a mystery. I think Slobodin and Rivers were a lot alike. In fact, in his book on Rivers, Slobodin (1978: 24) wrote: "There is a marked contrast between the photographs of Rivers taken in England and the pictures taken on various occasions in the field. In the home portraits, he appears buttoned-up, serious, and almost severe. The Melanesian pictures show him in tan shirt with open collar and rolled sleeves, bare feet in the sand, a relaxed posture and expression, and one of a close group."

I can't read this passage about Rivers without thinking of how it may also sum up Slobodin's stylistic double-sidedness. In reading Slobodin's rich interpretation of Rivers' personal life and of his intellectual work and political commitments, what is compelling is the tension between Rivers the formal, turn-of-the-century scholar and Rivers the rather more informal, almost liberated colleague while on the Torres Straits expeditions. Slobodin notes it and, in turn, I do too, in order to draw a parallel with Slobodin's own personality and personal and intellectual life history and style—between Slobodin's formalism and Slobodin's freedom. A projection of Rivers back onto Slobodin, to be sure, but as creative contagion, a force of the mimetic faculty as a dialectical image.

In interviewing Richard Slobodin, I would not so much have had an informant as an imaginative storyteller to listen to and stories and images on which to dwell. I never had the opportunity to ask Slobodin if he had ever read Walter Benjamin. I don't think he had. Isaiah Berlin and others like Berlin were more to his liking. Nevertheless, I think he would have found Benjamin's materialism, style of scholarship, and use of the dialectical image a challenge to the way he was thinking of our interview project and the kind of storytelling he was interested in exploring. Wishful thinking on my part, projection with a tinge of nostalgia, but a way to engage Slobodin now, a way back to the storyteller and to the freedom and power of storytelling; a way back also to his voice, its inflections, and his style of personal and intellectual engagement as example.

To relay events in a story, and then to retell stories in other versions, requires a close reading of forms—poetic attention. Slobodin's stories, stories about Slobodin, and exploring his double-sidedness would have made up the subject matter of my project. The narrative form of my project would have been to address Slobodin's immersion into the body of intertextual references to other stories, matters of fact, history, and how memory works on all of this. Every storyteller must be placed inside the story and yet also outside of it, constructing it; this is the haunting and double epistemology of speaking from within the object spoken of. As Ursula K. LeGuin (1981: 125) has argued, the function of such storytelling is "to bear witness, to leave a trace, to confer form onto life and finally to make survive." Tracking these traces closely and with care means tracking entangled stories as they are produced in dialogic addresses, imagined or real, and that draw our attention to the productive forms of such voices as an "act of becoming."[2]

That would be my job, to re-energize the act of storytelling to join Slobodin as storyteller and not betray the storyteller for the sake of what Benjamin called an illusory science of explanation. As he put it, the materialist project of history is not so much "to say" as "to show":

> The past can be seized only as an image which flashes up at an instant when it can be recognized and never seen again.... To articulate the past historically does not mean to recognize it "the way it really was" (Ranke). It means to seize hold of a memory as it flashes up at a moment of danger.... The danger affects both the content of the tradition and its receivers.... In every era the attempt must be made to wrest tradition away from conformism that is about to overpower it. (Benjamin, 1968: 255)

For me, this would mean crossing the divide, scary as it might be, and becoming a storyteller myself. As Slobodin, in conversation with Adelson (2001: 13), said, "Yes. You know how it is, once you get an old-time professor started, it's pretty hard to stop him. I could go on blabbing for a long time. But maybe we've had enough, eh?" The tragedy of this story is that we really never got started. So I find myself again perched nervously on a narrative edge, this time with the haunting fragments of an untold story of Slobodin as example.

NOTES

1 A footnote in Price's book makes reference to Charles Wagley's FBI foreign counter-intelligence file. Price found "a highly censored 'secret' document examining Wagely's association with radical and subversive individuals, which also makes mention of anthropologists Richard Slobodin.... The file indicates that the FBI investigated Slobodin after he published a letter in the *Daily People's World* (5/5/48) castigating the paper for obfuscating useful information through its heavy reliance on hyperbolistic jargon. The FBI read and catalogued the frequent mentions of anthropologist activities in the American Communist, Socialist, and progressive press" (2004: 373–74). And while I am on the subject of socially committed and Marxist anthropologists, Price (2004: 363) explains that the work and lives of "Gital Poznansky (Steed), Edward Haskell, Richard Slobodin, and Paul Robeson's wife, anthropologist Eslanda Robeson" are anthropologists who deserve much closer attention and "should provide good research subjects for future scholars."

2 For more on the poetics and politics of "becoming," see Rosi Braidotti (2002) and Brian Massumi (2002). Both scholars make important methodological moves that I think anthropology should begin to engage. For more on how a poetics of becoming combines with a dialogical approach, see Stewart (1996).

REFERENCES

Adelson, Naomi. 2001. "An Interview with Richard Slobodin on W.H.R. Rivers." In Michal Nahman, Naomi Adelson, and Gina Feldberg, eds., *Regeneration and Medical History: The Implications of "Fictionalized" Medicine for Teaching, Research, and Scholarship*. York University: York Centre for Health Studies.

Benjamin, Walter. 1968. "Theses on the Philosophy of History." In Hannah Arendt, ed., Harry Zohn, trans., *Illuminations*. New York: Schocken Books.

Braidotti, Rosi. 2002. *Metamorphoses: Towards a Materialist Theory of Becoming*. London: Polity Press.

LeGuin, Ursula K. 1981. "It Was a Dark and Stormy Night: or, Why Are We Huddling Around the Campfire?" In W.T.J. Mitchell, ed., *On Narrative*. Chicago: University of Chicago Press.

Massumi, Brian. 2002. *Parables for the Virtual: Movement, Affect, Sensation*. Durham, NC: Duke University Press.

Price, David. 2004. *Threatening Anthropology: McCarthyism and the FBI's Surveillance of Activist Anthropologists*. Durham, NC: Duke University Press.

Slobodin, Richard. 1978. *W.H.R. Rivers*. New York: Columbia University Press.

Stewart, Kathleen. 1996. *A Space on the Side of the Road: Cultural Poetics in an "Other" America*. Princeton, NJ: Princeton University Press.

CHAPTER FOUR

Writing against the Grain of Materialist Orthodoxy: Richard Slobodin and the Teetl'it Gwich'in

Robert Wishart and Michael Asch

In 1962 Richard Slobodin published a concise set of his observations on Gwich'in[1] social organization in *Band Organization of the Peel River Kutchin*, perhaps the most important monograph on the economy and society of the Dene, the people with whom we work. This essay will orient this publication within the context of current thinking (then more than now, but now as well) about the status of foraging in the modern world. It will show that Slobodin's careful representation of the Dene way of life in the late 1930s and the 1940s is a powerful and prescient critique of what would become anthropological orthodoxy, an orthodoxy that lends weight to the justification of colonial imposition, by turning what are relations of force into a process that seems natural and therefore just.

Both of us are part of a team that has been interrogating the relationship between anthropological theory and aboriginal rights. Concerned particularly with the role our orthodoxy has played in the colonial project in this country, we began with a question that some might think slanted and biased but that has proven to be productive for ourselves as well as for James Tully (2000), the political theorist who first posed it (albeit in a slightly different way). The question is: What causes our representations of the Indigenous to align so consistently with those emphasized by the colonial project?[2] Our first enquiry was into the materialists—and particularly Steward (although Murphy is implicated), Service, and Wolf—all of whom apply the concept of evolutionary development as the lens through which to represent foragers in the world today, including, specifically, Dene. Indeed, in North America these anthropologists make use of a representation of northern Aboriginal people's (particularly Athabascan and Algonquian) social organization and history in a remarkably consistent manner. Given limited space, we reduce what they have to say about Dene to two paradigmatic quotes. The first is by Murphy and Steward in *Tappers and Trappers* (1956: 353):

> When the people of an unstratified native society barter wild products found in extensive distribution and obtained through individual effort, the structure of native culture will be destroyed, and the final culmination will be a certain type characterized by individual families having delimited rights to marketable resources and linked to the larger nation through trading centres.

The second, by Elman Service in *Primitive Organization* (1962: 88–89), takes up the same theme:

> [Dene] who survived the early disasters [of contact] became employees (or, more accurately, dept-peons) of European fur-trading companies almost 200 years ago. The "peace of the market" has prevailed since the coming of Europeans to the subarctic, and bands as functional units have become mingled, indistinct, and unimportant. Before this, it is clear, warfare among unrelated groups had been an enormously important consideration in causing firm residential entities, marriage alliances among them, and the formation of adult male sodalities for defence as well as hunting—all of which cause strong social divisions as well as bond and militate against the kind of amorphous organization called "composite."

In short, it is an image of the triumph of capital over the foraging mode of production, a triumph that may arrive quickly (as in Service's view) or through a longer evolutionary process (as in Murphy and Steward). But it is a triumph that is, nonetheless, an inevitability.

In anthropological theorizing, it is the continued privileging of this kind of account, notably in Wolf's *Europe and the People without History* (1982), that provides the linkage between our representations and the colonial project of which we speak. If Richard Slobodin ever internalized this account, he should be credited for seeing beyond it. Certainly, he was immersed in an anthropological world that would have made it comfortable to proceed from Steward's and Service's positions. He was a graduate student at Columbia at the beginning of its Golden Age as the leading institution in materialist anthropology. Although he completed his dissertation in 1959, years later than others, his contemporaries included Diamond, Fried, Harris, Leacock, Manners, Murphy, and Wolf, the generation that was to establish materialism's hegemonic moment. He was certainly aware of the direction it was taking, and with it the picture of foraging that was to become dominant.

Notwithstanding the soon-to-be orthodoxy about the process of cultural change developing among his contemporaries and his location at its centre, Slobodin chose to take another stance. Slobodin's monograph on Gwich'in band organization is based on his dissertation (1959) and asserts that, while the ecological evolutionary theory espoused by Steward (1955) and his students has merit in taking into consideration the ecological constraints placed on social organization and economics, the presumption that the Gwich'in economy is thereby decimated is disconfirmed by what he observed and was told in the field about the current circumstances of Dene economy and society.

Writing against the grain but from within a materialist paradigm, Slobodin situates the key discrepancy between their theory and his observations in economic factors, and particularly in the status of foraging as a mode of production in the face of capitalist expansion. He therefore accepts the basic premise that ecology is important in the reckoning of a mode of production in northern Canada while bringing to light conscious decision-making among Gwich'in actors, thereby distancing him from the stimulus–response inevitability of the prevailing myth of what occurs when a foraging mode of production comes face to face with capitalism.

To the presumptions of the Stewardians, Slobodin replies in the introduction of his book (1962: 5):

> The history of the Peel River Kutchin in recent generations has not been that of a people who "helplessly accept the conqueror's ways, or passively die out, or go down fighting with the spear or the gun," nor yet has there been a "moral regeneration" in a nativistic movement. These types of eventuality have been great concern to the anthropologist. Yet it is felt that a distinctive contribution may be made from the study of a people who actively maintain a hunting economy, who display considerable *esprit de corps*, and whose social forms show at once the mark of tradition and a capacity for adaptation to current situations.

He then proceeds in detail to explore the history of contact to create what becomes a powerful and often not subtle critique of the orthodoxy. Slobodin substantiates his argument that the Gwich'in actively maintain a hunting economy by providing a plethora of observations that contradict the "eventuality" materialist theory, of which we will mention three: (1) that the Gwich'in made conscious decisions about how or if they will participate in imported economic activities such as the fur trade and the gold rush and organized themselves accordingly, (2) that trapping is a form of hunting, and (3) that either forced or coerced settlement in frontier towns with economies based on wage labour coupled with a loss of jurisdiction over their lands has the greatest potential for creating the conditions for negative aspects of culture change.

Slobodin's description of Gwich'in economic activities positions him against the same static view of culture that formed the basis of the materialist critique of earlier anthropological depictions. Indeed, he argues that it is full of what he refers to as "shifts," "developments of interest," and "strategies," all of which he relates to conscious decisions tempered by Gwich'in ideals (1962: 33). He points out that there are a number of ecological-economic factors that "stimulate" shifts in economic emphasis, including the price of fur in general and the difference in the price of furs between marten, muskrat, and beaver, and the availability of caribou along different points of their migration routes. All of these factors feature in Gwich'in decision-making at the various levels of individual, family, band, and tribe. Furthermore, he shows that, contrary to the pattern theorized by Steward (1955), cultures are not determined by a single dominant techno-environmental adaptation but by decisions people make under different conditions. By incorporating consciousness and social relations of production, he describes a pattern of social organization that is almost the opposite of Steward's. When resources are scarce, most Gwich'in choose to congregate and assist each other (1962: 69, 80, 83), thus confirming that, for them, the mutual-assistance and the power of social relationships are important factors in the relations of production. As one of Slobodin's Gwich'in teachers argued: "Indians don't have a bank ... but the people, the Peel River people is like a bank for us. You work all your life and help other people, and when you get old everybody helps you" (1962: 68).

Conversely, during times of greater abundance in resources, the Gwich'in choose between various elements of their diverse economy and spread out over their lands with some "parties" hunting upriver, some in the mountains, and some focusing their efforts on the delta country. These "parties" are governed by a set of values that include a "high valuation of individual competence in subsistence activity," "high valuation of physical and social mobility," "desire to associate with persons of high status," which has been assigned according to expertise, and the "importance of group membership ... and fear of solitude and of the solitary" (1962: 84–85).

As for the impact of cultural contact, Slobodin argues that the Stewardian materialists' myopia about the impact of capital led them to underemphasize the continuing importance of foraging in their model. During the fur trade, Slobodin shows that trapping had to be considered as being compatible, rather than in conflict, with hunting. This important observation is based on a detailed discussion of facts such as these. First, for most of the fur trade history, the posts—like the gold seekers—were dependent upon the Gwich'in for food. Fort McPherson, like other trade posts on Dene lands, was primarily a "meat camp" until the advent of steamships on the northwestern rivers in the late 1800s (1962: 22). Second, then as now, fur trapping involves more than participation in a market economy. The killing of muskrat and beaver is also a subsistence activity and contributed to the caloric intake of Gwich'in to the point where some that chose to pursue muskrat hunting were referred to as "rat-eaters" (1962: 40). Moreover, there is a subsistence pattern even when Gwich'in trap animals that they do not normally consume as food as trapping is combined with other foraging pursuits: marten trapping combined with caribou and moose hunting, beaver and muskrat trapping and hunting combined with rabbit snaring, moose hunting, duck and goose hunting, and riverine fishing (1962: 22–23, 82–83), to name just a few activities. Third, Slobodin describes the set of skills and knowledge that are used in trapping as being a form of hunting. Finally, trapping requires access to and travel over Gwich'in lands by the hunters and trappers (1962: 83).

Slobodin's description in "Life with a Trapping Party" (1962: 47–53) evidences his argument that trapping for the world fur market is far more complex than a simple conquering of original economy and culture and certainly represents something far more than the survival attempts of refugees. Indeed, trapping for the world fur market is an introduced system, but it does not subsume the foraging mode of production as described by Murphy and Steward. In fact, Slobodin's description is of a relatively stable social life with a dominant foraging economy that includes production for capital markets as an activity, a situation later confirmed by Asch (1976, 1977, 1979, 1982), Rushforth (1977), Savishinsky (1976), Smith (1976), Usher (1976), and presented as evidence at the Mackenzie Valley Pipeline hearings (Berger, 1977: xix). There are a few important observations that Slobodin makes during this trip that deserve further elaboration and attention.

First, the trip that Slobodin took in the late winter of 1947 was a cooperative effort of twenty-five individuals belonging to five "families" travelling together into the Richardson Mountains. While Slobodin (1962: 48) describes a group of this size travelling together to set up a marten-trapping camp as unusual and occurring only once in several years, setting up trapping camps is still a common occurrence. Today, members from what could be seen as different nuclear families may decide to camp together for the purpose of foraging. However, then as now, when members of different families come together they refer to each other using kin terms "as though they constituted a bilateral extended family" (1962; 48). His description of how other groups may decide to join in at a later date and still be incorporated (1962: 53) is particularly apt in the present situation, where travel is made easier with the use of mechanized transport (Wishart, 2004). The importance of incorporating people into an extended kin system when engaged in a "market" economic activity such as trapping is a key element in Slobodin's questioning of the inevitability of culture change resulting from market-driven activities in the formation of "individual families" (Murphy and Steward, 1956).

Second, the stated purpose of this trip was to trap marten for the fur trade; however, it became apparent to Slobodin that this activity was to be combined with the "main subsistence activities, moose and caribou hunting," along with rabbit snaring (1962: 47). In fact, more than half of Slobodin's description of the activities of this trapping party relates to hunting for caribou and moose. To this day, what people say the trip is about does not necessarily describe the activities taking place, with hunting often taking up much of the time and effort. Therefore, the term "trapping" can be used fairly broadly in Gwich'in country to describe an economic pursuit that is just part of a much larger body of economic activities that take place on the land, including hunting, snaring, fishing, woodcutting, and plant gathering for food and medicine. This problem of outsiders not knowing what "trapping" entails was part of Berger's argument (1977: 110) that Dene hunting economies had been misrepresented as subsumed by the trapping economy.

Third is Slobodin's evocative description of the coexistence of differing forms of ownership. He describes a situation that arises when trapping and then couples it with a description of a cooperative moose hunt. First, the trapping description:

> Stephen[3] brought a marten back on the evening of the following day, the first full day's intensive trapping. It had been caught in one of several traps which he had found set by people who had passed along the Eagle several weeks earlier. Amazingly, the pelt was intact. Stephen did what any passing trappers would do; he skinned and stretched the pelt, thereby saving it from destruction by wolves or wolverines.

> In the course of the winter, Stephen would probably come across the owner of the trap which had caught the marten. If not, he would sell the fur at Easter and give or send the proceeds to the owner when his identity was

learned. This is the usual procedure when one discovers a fur animal in a trap not set on a known trap-line. (1962: 50)

This description is quickly followed by his account of a moose hunt that occurred a few days after the marten-trapping event:

> Just after dark on the sixth day at the camp, Mark Lawrence saw moose signs. This was welcome news, for although the women and children had been snaring rabbits, no large game had been seen, and the small supply of "proper" meat—i.e., caribou or moose—was almost exhausted.

> That evening Stephen remarked to me, "Now you will see how we go hunting in a bunch the right way." Moses [an elder] illustrated the procedure with several hunting stories. It turned out, indeed, that the plan of the hunt accorded well with Moses' account of hunting in his heyday....

> [After cooperative tracking of the moose, it was shot and killed by Willie.] When Stephen and I arrived, Willie and Mark Lawrence were butchering the moose. Several men had gone back for their toboggans and teams, in order to haul the meat. Willie presented the moose on the spot to Mark Lawrence, who returned half the skin to Willie and gave the head to Stephen. Most of the meat was apportioned among the heads of the families on the basis of family size....

> As was expected of him, Mark Lawrence contributed most of his share of meat for a generous communal supper that evening. (1962: 51–52)

What becomes apparent from this account is that it is true that trapping leads to a different form of ownership. The pelt of the marten belongs to the person who sets the trap. While in this case he says that the pelt belongs to the owner of the trap, Slobodin is careful to document elsewhere (1962: 50) that the pelt does not *necessarily* belong to the person who owns the trap. In one case, a few younger trappers were learning about trapping marten from one of the more experienced trappers and it was understood that the fur from the first few days of trapping belonged to the teacher regardless of who owned the traps they were caught in. However, there is a clear sense that when Gwich'in visit the trading post to sell their furs, it is on an individual basis, although even this is fairly recent—in the past, the furs were pooled and traded by a trading chief to Europeans who would then distribute the goods. It was only with great expenditure by the Hudson's Bay Company in moving the posts further into Gwich'in country, then trying to adequately supply them an develop relationships with individual families, that the company was able to break this monopoly and trade directly with the heads of the families (1962: 59).

Slobodin then presents the reader with an account of a moose hunt that is, according to the elder, the "right way" to hunt. Not only does this description give us a sense of the importance of hunting for big game by the men while trapping, but it also gives us a glimpse of another important economic activity, the snaring and hunting of small game by everyone. Indeed, while in the mountains the contribution to the foraging economy of snared and hunted rabbits, ptarmigan, and grouse can easily be over- · looked, but the meat from these animals is what often feeds the trappers. When big game such as moose are successfully hunted by a party of hunters, there is still a sense of ownership, the moose is given by the man who shot and killed it to the man who first saw the signs and planned the hunt. He then distributes the meat among everyone and holds a feast to further distribute his share. This is a practice that continues to this day.

What Slobodin describes is a group of people who travel together and are able to trap furs together with the understanding that the constraints of the structure of the fur-trade post means that they must sell their furs individually. However, in all the other economic activities during the trip the foraging economic rules prevail. The people are able to work within their own economy to make room for trading, but it in no way dominates the structure of the total economy. In fact, what Slobodin does not really report on is what becomes of the goods bought with the furs. In our experience, some of the goods purchased are luxuries that are partially consumed by the trapper and his family and some are given away and redistributed in a similar fashion as the moose meat, but a good deal of the goods return to the reciprocal foraging economy in the form of hunting supplies (Asch, 1982: 363).

Slobodin argued that Gwich'in maintained their economic autonomy even in times of intense contact, such as during the Yukon gold rush, showing that Gwich'in who chose to participate in it did so within a pre-existing Gwich'in economy of hunting. As Slobodin describes, they certainly had many adventures with the dramatically increased contact with outsider gold seekers,[4] but despite this potential for dramatic change to the Gwich'in economy, the actual nature of the experience was non-traumatic. "During the gold rush," he says, "there was no winter activity more profitable than hunting, and as the mining locations were within easy reach of the traditional Peel River hunting grounds, hunting in the mountains continued as the principal winter occupation" (1962: 84).

Slobodin then enquires into the factors that produced this history, deciding that the hunting economy has enough "flexibility" to show "viability and vitality" (1962: 86–87) to deal with even the most intense forms of contact as long as the following additional permissive conditions are met. The first is the "(r)etention" of the "pre-contact habitat" (1962: 84), which he means are the right and ability of Gwich'in to exercise considerable choice over the activities on their lands. The second is the ability of Gwich'in to at times participate in both wage labour and in the hunting economy. The third is the establishment of frontier towns on the periph-ery of Gwich'in lands, placing the Gwich'in beyond the more forceful or coercive state efforts to revolutionize the Gwich'in way of life, thus mak-ing the choice between participating in either the wage or the hunting economy possible. Of these three, it is only the last one that time has shown to be incorrect. As the work we have done with our respective Dene communities—Asch in the 1970s and 1980s and Wishart in the 1990s and early 2000s—even the forced move into permanent sites within such towns has not overwhelmed the foraging economy.

In sum, *Band Organization of the Peel River Kutchin* provides a robust refutation of the story of cultural change that Slobodin's colleagues and teachers told. It is a story that was repeated by our Dene instructors when discussing historical events with them during our respective fieldwork in the 1970s and 1980s and 1990s and early 2000s and when discussed with other Athapaskanists as well. It was confirmed in the report of the Macken-zie Valley Pipeline Inquiry, in which Justice Berger (1977: 110–13) found that evidence on the continued importance of foraging refuted the propo-sition that, using language that could have been written by Murphy and Steward (1956), the jobs this mega-project would create were a benefit that outweighed other impacts because it would ease the Dene's painful transition from an economy that remained in the Stone Age to one that made them a part of the Space Age. Therefore, he recommended a ten-year moratorium on its construction during which developmental assistance should be provided so that, as through the development of a capacity to process furs in the North, Dene would be able to participate in that econ-omy to the fullest extent possible.

It is well beyond the scope of this paper to delve into the reasons that Slobodin's colleagues maintained their vision of culture contact in the face of his clear refutation,[5] much less to attempt to explain, as has been the topic of our research thus far, why it continues to be privileged in the face of overwhelming evidence that it is a fantasy. What Slobodin's work reveals is that the narrative that the materialist literature tells about culture con-tact could not have been sustained had his reports, written with such clar-ity and fidelity to fact, been taken into account. That is really a disappointment, for, had the ideas about change that he presented in the early 1960s been integrated into the narrative, rather than erased, the chances are that materialism would have become less of a perspective that sustains the colonizer's image of the condition of the Indigenous in the modern world, and more of a place from which to resist it.

Nothing could make this point more clearly than the following anecdote. During his first summer of fieldwork with the Teetlit Gwich'in, Rob Wishart was seen by Eileen Koe reading about the relationship between the Gwich'in and European fur traders. Eileen is an elder from whom he would go on in subsequent years to learn a great deal. On this occasion, Rob was reading a piece that contained descriptions of contact between Gwich'in and European traders. On finding him reading it, Eileen exclaimed: "That is all bullshit." Later that week, she handed him *Band Organization of the Peel River Kutchin* and told him that it "got things better." Three words that attest more eloquently than those we write here that Richard Slobodin's body of work is of the highest quality and integrity; it is work that commands our deference and respect.

NOTES

1 Following the convention of the time, Slobodin spelled Gwich'in as "Kutchin." For a treatise on the history of Gwich'in ethnonyms and variations in spelling, see Wishart (2004).
2 Tully's questions (200: 36; emphasis his) are: "How does political theory hinder or help the liberation of indigenous peoples? That is, in what ways can political theory help or hinder the struggles of indigenous peoples *for* and *of* freedom?"
3 Slobodin uses pseudonyms throughout his work on Gwich'in.
4 During the height of the Yukon gold rush, Dawson City had a larger population than Vancouver.
5 Consider, for example, that Service (1962) did not reference Slobodin's 1959 Ph.D. dissertation on Dene social structure but referenced instead Fathauer's 1942 M.A. thesis.

REFERENCES

Asch, Michael. 1976. "Some Effects of the Late Ninteenth-Century Modernization of the Fur Trade on the Economy of the Slavey Indians." *Western Canadian Journal of Anthropology* 6(4): 7–15.
——. 1977. "The Dene Economy." In Mel Watkins, ed., *Dene Nation: The Colony Within*. Toronto: University of Toronto Press.
——. 1979. "The Ecological-Evolutionary Model and the Concept of Mode of Production." In David H. Turner and Gavin A. Smith, eds., *Challenging Anthropology*. Toronto: McGraw-Hill Ryerson.
——. 1982. "Dene Self-Determination and the Study of Hunter-Gatherers in the Modern World." In Eleanor Leacock and Richard Lee, eds., *Politics and History in Band Societies*. Cambridge: Cambridge University Press.

Berger, Thomas. 1977. *Northern Frontier Northern Homeland: Report of the Mackenzie Valley Pipeline Inquiry*. Ottawa: Printing and Publishing Supply and Services Canada.

Fathauer, George. 1942. "Social Organisation and Kinship of the Northern Athabaskan Indians." M.A. thesis, University of Chicago.

Murphy, Robert, and Julian Steward. 1956. "Tappers and Trappers: Parallel Process in Acculturation." *Economic Development and Culture Change* 4(4): 335–55.

Rushforth, Scott. 1977. "Country Food." In Mel Watkins, ed., *Dene Nation: The Colony Within*. Toronto: University of Toronto Press.

Savishinsky, Joel. 1976. Untiltiled Brief submitted to the Mackenzie Valley Pipeline Inquiry. "Records of the Mackenzie Valley Pipeline Inquiry." Exhibit no. 645.

Service, Elman. 1962. *Primitive Social Organization: An Evolutionary Perspective*. Random House: New York.

Slobodin, Richard. 1959. "Band Organization of the Peel River Kutchin." Ph.D. dissertation, Columbia University.

———. 1962. *Band Organization of the Peel River Kutchin*. National Museum of Canada Bulletin No. 179. Ottawa: Northern Affairs and National Resources.

Smith, James. 1976. "Local Band Organisation of the Caribou-eater Chipewyan." *Arctic Anthropology* 13(1): 12–24.

Steward, Julian. 1955. *The Theory of Culture Change: The Methodology of Multilinear Evolution*. Urbana: University of Illinois Press.

Tully, James. 2000. "The Struggles of Indigenous Peoples for and of Freedom." In D. Iveseon, P. Patton, and W. Sanders, eds., *Political Theory and the Rights of Indigenous Peoples*, 36–59. Cambridge: Cambridge University Press.

Usher, Peter J. 1976. "Evaluating Country Food in the Northern Native Economy." *Arctic* 29(2): 105–20.

Wishart, Robert. 2004. "Living 'On the Land': Teetl'it Gwich'in Perspectives on Continuities." Ph.D. dissertation, University of Alberta.

Wolf, Eric. 1982. *Europe and the People without History*. Berkeley: University of California Press.

CHAPTER FIVE

Histories of the Past, Histories of the Future: The Committed Anthropologies of Richard Slobodin, Frank G. Speck, and Eleanor Leacock

Harvey A. Feit[1]

It is a misty two-dimensional world. A number of objects in varying shapes of black and grey are moving irregularly across a field of white. It is not easy to determine the identity of these shapes; how many there are, or even in what direction they are moving. Then slowly the picture comes into focus.

It is a mountain valley above treeline. In the half-light of an Arctic winter, wolves and men are pursuing caribou. They are competitors. The wolves are trying to isolate a deer or two from the rest of the herd. The men curse the wolves for scattering the prey and "running their fat off." Both man and wolf, at this season of the year, are dependent for their lives upon the flesh of these gregarious ruminants. Predators both, they worry the herd as do the warble flies which infest the caribou in summer.

The uncertain light, the difficulty in perception, seems appropriate, for is this not a scene from "the dawn of history"? Is it not a museum diorama, an animated Mousterian landscape?

In point of fact, it is a scene from our times. The glacial era has passed. These are contemporary mammals. The men—in whom we are most interested—subscribe to newspapers, own radios, use the latest model hunting rifles. They are a hunting people, but they are vitally concerned by the pressures of the modern world. (Slobodin, 1962: 1)

This literary evocation opened Richard Slobodin's 1962 monograph, recalling the surprising connections and disjunctures one encounters in the field, the complexities of perception and understanding, and the importance of location and of time. He cautions about the need to examine and consider time and history carefully. In this setting, the images one brings may lead one to seek to connect and possibly confuse contemporary hunters with hunters of millennia past or with those in museums of the last century. He thus graphically recalls and problematizes history as a set of ideas that we bring with us and that are embedded in our perceptions, even after the picture of what we think we are observing comes into focus. As I explore below, he raises questions about how we link these hunters to our histories of humankind, and he highlights the complexities we encounter in trying to acknowledge their full agency in their histories and in our own.

The ethnographic present of Dick Slodobin's word picture is his 1946–47 doctoral fieldwork—and the literary introduction was commented on by some reviewers of his 1962 monograph for its distinctiveness at the time of its publication (e.g., Osgood, 1963: 944). His erudite and challenging focus on the need for ethnographies and histories, and for the careful consideration of history and agency, is taken up as the theme of this chapter.

Dick's focus was not only on history as event and history as stories and ideas but on the interplay of colonial, market, and local structures in histories. The theme of structures and history was a topic coming to prominence in anthropology in the post–Second World War period. At the time there was the rise of ethnohistory with its complications of historical methodologies, of cultural ecology with its focus on structures of cultures in context, and of structuralism and the debates it generated over its relations to history. The introduction to Slobodin's monograph can be read as an invitation to explore the ways that structures and histories are intertwined. In the monograph itself, his interests range from social organization to ecology, from world fur markets to the ideas of "Western civilization" and progress, from the historical limits anticipated and futures of hunting peoples to the happenstance, chaotic, and specific constraints on Gwich'in.

I want to highlight his contributions to these discussions by setting his study in the context of how two of his contemporaries were using history and the analyses of structures in the period before and after the Second World War. I focus on Frank G. Speck and Eleanor Leacock, who worked in the eastern subarctic and whose work Slobodin cited. I show how each of these three sought in different ways to develop histories of subarctic peoples that stood outside the accepted self-histories of American and Canadian societies, and especially those histories that made subarctic peoples marginal or victimized. I show how each sought to develop what we would today call committed and engaged anthropology.

All three were critics, but they were critics in different and sometimes conflicting ways. Each of them worked "against the grain" of colonialism rooted in a mainstream social evolutionary theory and history. Speck envisaged subarctic hunters as agents of their own development, and he asserted the possibility of a future that was not evolutionary or assimilated but based on "tradition" and the land. For Leacock, subarctic hunters' histories were defined by the effects of, and the alternatives to, capitalism and colonial domination. Grounded in a radical evolutionism, she systematically portrayed how market trade was changing subarctic hunters and what of value was being lost. The implication in her early work at least was that what was hopeful in their future would be tied to more general radical social struggles. Slobodin saw a past filled with the agency of hunters operating within historical structures that were not entirely of their own making, and futures that would be more uncertain and probably more unexpected, albeit still structured by living on the land, the constraining effects of colonizing outsiders and markets, as well as by people's own stories and visions.

PROFESSIONAL INTERESTS AND CONTEXTS

Following the vivid introduction to *Band Organization of the Peel River Kutchin* (1962), which was based on his Ph.D. dissertation, Dick went on to emphasize his interest in the intersection of social organization, environment, economy, and history in the social sciences of the time. Dick noted that research on hunting and gathering societies had been "motivated in great part by historical interest" (1962: 1). He noted that Julian Steward had in the recent two decades addressed himself to analyses of band societies and to "both general process and to specific historical sequence" (1962: 2, referencing Steward's 1936 and 1955 publications, which bracketed Dick's own early northern travel and later fieldwork). Thus, Dick noted that the "study of primary-group formation and structure among peoples in hunting and gathering economies is of interest both as part of ethnohistory and as a prerequisite to any theory of culture history, evolutionary or other" (1962: 2).

Dick argued that among studies of hunting and gathering peoples, the "material on the northeastern Algonkian-speaking Indians of the Labrador

peninsula" must be used and taken into account by "any student of cultural development" (1962: 2).[2] The debates over the form of the family
in early Algonquian societies, and over the impacts of the fur trade and market institutions on Algonquian tenure systems and social organization,
were central to the conflicts within the discipline between Boasian culture historians and evolutionary theorists, mainly those who referred back
to Marx and Engels and to Morgan but also those evolutionists who
referred back to Darwin, Spencer, and Sumner.

In his introduction, Dick cited diverse Algonquianist scholars involved
in these debates, including Frank G. Speck, W. Duncan Strong, John
Cooper, Julius Lips, Loren Eiseley, and Eleanor Leacock (1962: 2–3). He
noted in particular how Eleanor Leacock had combined field data with historical documentation and how, in contrast, opportunities for historical
research on other peoples of northern North America "are only beginning to be realized." He emphasized that "the use of historical material has
not been much in evidence for the northern Athapaskans" (1962: 3). This
was a task he set out to address.

He also made clear that his interest in history was not limited to analyzing the classic concerns of culture trait sequences or the most common
models of market-induced socio-economic transformations or acculturation. He said he was "not concerned with acculturation to western civilization, nor with distinctions between 'aboriginal' and 'borrowed' culture
traits" (1962: 3–4).

Dick's interests included particular and individual lives and roles, but
they were also generalizing, and they were thoroughly processual. He
asked,

> What have been the discernable regularities in the kinds of [social] group-
> ings found among this people during its known history? How—that is, on
> what principles of organization— may these regularities be generalized?
> We would then wish to ascertain whether the phenomena of group organ-
> ization can be explained by conditions of an ecological order (e.g., recur-
> rent variations) and by those of a historical order (non-recurrent
> variation).... Persistence cannot be taken for granted. It should be possi-
> ble, given sufficient data, to attempt an explanation of it, as well as of
> change. (1962: 4)

Although Dick modestly presented this work, it could be viewed as a broad
project to explore new ways that historical analyses could be incorporated
into hunter and gatherer research and, more generally, how historical studies needed not just to contribute to but to question and problematize wider
debates on evolution, acculturation, and tradition.

I explore his contribution by examining the role that historical analyses and stories played in the works of Frank G. Speck and Eleanor Leacock, and how Slobodin's work can be read as responding to and greatly expanding the analytical and agentive histories that they explored. His contributions to these debates have not been widely recognized.

SPECK'S CHANGING HISTORIES OF ALGONQUIAN TENURE, "WESTERN" DESTINY, AND INDIGENOUS AGENCY

One of the central examples in the long-standing debates about evolution and history in the first half of the twentieth century was about eastern subarctic hunter-gatherer social organization and tenure.

In an earlier paper I showed how advocacy shaped Frank G. Speck's presentations of the ethnography of family hunting territory systems and his claim that they were "the basis of American Indian ownership of the land" (Speck, 1914, 1915a, 1915c; Hallowell, 1951: 73; also Hallowell, 1949: 35; Feit, 1991a; Deschênes, 1981; Pulla, 2003). Here, I briefly recall that period in order to go on to analyze what Speck did after 1918, once his initial academic articles were published.

Speck argued in opposition to major policy-makers who used in part Darwinian social evolutionary models in their policies, and later against scholars working from the Marxist evolutionary tradition. In his 1914 article, Speck rebutted Theodore Roosevelt's claim that

> [t]o recognize Indian ownership of the limitless prairies and forests of this continent (that is, to consider the dozen squalid savages who hunted at long intervals over a territory of a thousand square miles, as owning it outright) necessarily implies a similar recognition of the claims of every white hunter, squatter, horse thief, or wandering cattleman. (T. Roosevelt, "The Winning of the West," cited in Speck, 1914: 35)

Speck claimed Roosevelt was wrong and unjust, and he presented his own findings on Algonquian hunting territory systems in reply. The argument was related to the process in which Roosevelt and his government were involved—namely, the transfer of vast tracts of land and natural resources from indigenous control to private or government control. This was being done through programs that allotted indigenous and treaty lands to private individuals and by the progressive conservation policies that placed major natural resources under government as opposed to local management in order to better serve national economic interests (see Feit, 1991a). Both were legitimated in part by the asserted evolutionary superiority of the modern institutions of European and American societies and polities, and particularly the values of private property, governmental expertise, and scientific management. Both programs were founded in evolutionary historical stories of the progress of non-native Americans (see, for example, Hays, 1969 [1959], on progressive conservationism, and Hoxie, 1984, on allotment).

Speck was presenting an alternative to these views when he argued that Algonquian hunting territories were a means of game conservation founded on private property ownership of land among a hunting and gathering people. He initially described the family hunting group as a kinship group based on consanguineal and affinal ties that had "the right to hunt, trap and fish in a certain inherited district bounded by some rivers, lakes, and other natural landmarks"(1915c: 290; see also 1915b). The hunting districts, or territories, were "owned from time immemorial by the same families and handed down from generation to generation" (1915c: 290). Territoriality allowed owners to keep close account of the resources, and the killing of game was "definitely regulated so that only the increase is consumed, enough stock being left each season to insure a supply for the succeeding year. In this manner the game is 'farmed,' so to speak ..." (1915c: 293).

Later ethnographers have clearly shown that Speck was wrong to think the Algonquian hunting territory systems were forms of private property, but they have confirmed that hunting territories were often related to practices that achieved effective conservation (see Tanner, 1979; Scott, 1979, 1986, 1988; Feit, 1973, 1982, 1991b, and see 2005 for a review). Speck's efforts to argue that indigenous peoples already had private property in some form, and that they were conservationists, were part of careerlong arguments he made against the assumed inevitable demise of indigenous peoples (see Deschênes, 1981; Feit, 1991a).[3]

Despite Speck's efforts to influence the governments of the U.S., Canada, and Quebec to establish new policies that legally recognized Algonquian hunting territories and gave them exclusive rights to the wildlife on those lands (see Feit, 1991a; Pulla, 2003), these arguments failed to influence policy-makers. Speck's policy-oriented work was acknowledged by Gifford Pinchot, the forester, crusader, and former policy-maker who initiated government conservation institutions and programs under Roosevelt. When Pinchot gave a talk at the University of Pennsylvania Houston Club in 1919, he titled the address "The Use of the Natural Resources by the Indians." The archived drafts of his talk include a copy with the note "This copy contains corrections made by Prof. Speck about April 1, 1919"; the note was written four days before the talk was delivered (Pinchot Papers, Library of Congress, Manuscripts Division). Pinchot spent most of his talk acknowledging and reporting on Speck's findings, including quotes from Speck's account of hunting territories as a system of conservation. As well, he cited several other anthropological examples, all of which were in sharp contrast to the views expressed in 1914 by Roosevelt:

> Long before the first white man set foot in America, the conservation of certain natural resources was most carefully practiced among the Indian tribes of what is now the Northeastern part of the United States, as professor Frank G. Speck of the University of Pennsylvania was first to show.... To the Indian, Prof. Speck well says, there was no wilderness. Trackless to the whites, to him all the land was known and within the limitations set by his knowledge of natural resources all of it was used. (Pinchot [1919])

Pinchot thus recognized indigenous conservation practices, based largely on Speck's work, and he said that not only were indigenous peoples conservationists but they were also "progressive conservationists," that is, they made as much use of resources as they could, which he valued.

But this recognition was qualified, because he also claimed that their efforts were constrained by their limited knowledge (Pinchot, [1919]). The final version of the unpublished paper included a claim that "natives realize the hopelessness of conserving their resources where they have to compete with the avarice of white frontiersmen" (Pinchot Papers, Library of Congress, Manuscripts Division). He thereby asserted that in the contemporary context there was a need for government ownership, regulation, and control, as opposed to leaving lands and resources under indigenous ownership and stewardship. He also asserted that indigenous peoples "realized" this inevitability.

Thus, while Speck succeeded in gaining some recognition that indigenous peoples were conservationists, this was not sufficient. The historical inevitability of non-native control of the resources was necessitated by non-native avarice, which required modern government intervention.

Another implicit critique of Speck's work on Indian land ownership by policy-makers was published in a 1926 issue of the alumni magazine at the University of Pennsylvania, where Speck was on the faculty. This issue carried a group of articles on "assimilating the red man," one of which was by George Vaux of the U.S. Federal Indian Bureau. He argued that "tribes" were insufficiently developed and had limited need of land, pointing out that "distinct tribes might have particular areas which they claimed to own but that ownership was not land-tenure of the kind we

Anglo-Saxons have developed." He went on to say, echoing Roosevelt, that "a few hundreds of thousands of strolling people hunting and fishing—here to-day and somewhere else to-morrow, with no continuing fixed places of abode, necessarily could not have the ideas of ownership which we have, nor ... could they be considered as owning that land in the same sense of making any real use of it" (Vaux, 1926: 101).

Speck's article "Annihilating the Indian," in the next issue of the journal, noted that these plans for the amelioration of the Indian problems were being discussed in the absence or "exclusion of possible native points of view from the range of consideration," and he also made a plea for the use of ethnology and evidence (Speck, 1926a: 262). Speck pointed out that he had noted a similar argument in the conclusion of his 1915 paper, titled "Basis of American Indian Ownership of the Land": "I emphasized the application of this information, hoping that it would reach the attention of those in authority in Indian affairs, for whom it was intended as an aid in their handling of the situation,—an expectation not realized in the case of Mr. Vaux, who illustrates the indifference in [*sic*] the part of the administrators toward ethnological facts" (Speck, 1926a: 267–69, cited in Feit 1991: 124n4).

Speck again addressed policy issues in print in 1936, two decades after his initial publications, accusing Indian agents and administrations in Canada and the U.S. of being ignorant of the indigenous system of tenure. In one passage he proposed as a remedy that the Indian bureaus insert questions on indigenous land tenure into the Indian civil service examination for potential appointees (1936: 149).

A part of this article was written as if it were a memorandum "to the authorities of the Indian Department of the Dominion of Canada to whose attention it may by chance come" (Speck, 1936: 155). In addressing a crisis among the Montagnais living on the north shore of the St. Lawrence, Speck advised that if they were to be assisted in improving their economic and health conditions, it would be best to avoid outside intrusion or "social protection" but rather stabilize the "bush" food supply within its natural conditions (1936: 155). To achieve this he prescribed that non-natives be barred from hunting and trapping inland from the coast, and that the government should "make over to the natives of the interior barrens of the Labrador peninsula an inalienable legal title to what is left of their inherited domain where they can operate their age-old institutions of game farming and conservation and family-group or communal hunting, as the case may be, guaranteeing their economic future" (Speck, 1936: 159, echoing Cooper [1933]; see also Feit, 2005).

Such a policy of limiting non-native intrusions would have responded to claims like those of Pinchot, that indigenous conservation was doomed by the inevitable expansion of non-natives and the latter's avarice. Here governments are called on to support indigenous rights by placing limits on non-native avarice and expansion rather than by taking over indigenous lands.

In these and other cases, Speck's solutions to the Indian policy dilemmas had ephemeral effects on the policy debates he was addressing, as far as we know, and this is reflected in the absence of references to Speck's advice in histories of these conservation policies. Nevertheless, Speck himself remained intermittently active in policy arenas throughout his career, although he also showed frustration at his limited influence and became skeptical and sometimes cynical about policy-making.[4]

Speck was thus a continuing critical anthropological voice calling for involvement of indigenous peoples in policy-making, as well as bringing the relevance of ethnography into policy. While he himself declined to serve directly as an adviser, he nevertheless continued to write public policy commentaries and unofficial memoranda on policy issues (for earlier examples of his policy interventions, see Feit, 1991a). He carried these same commitments into his academic publications, from 1915 to the 1940s.

Within academia Speck's arguments for the historical depth and continuity, and therefore legal precedence, of indigenous peoples' systems of tenure and conservation were also challenged. This was done mainly by scholars who defended evolutionary models, whether of Darwinian or Marxist influence, and whether the scholars were defenders of indigenous peoples' rights and aspirations or not. For example, prominent among the early opponents in Canada was Diamond Jenness, who worked at the National Museum of Canada and who succeeded Edward Sapir as Canada's chief ethnologist. Jenness was often a critic of government's indigenous policies, but he also served periodically as a policy adviser or commentator between the 1940s and the early 1960s. Jenness's research in the 1920s and 1930s on the Sekani and on the Ojibwa documented the impact of the fur trade, which led him to conclude that hunting territories were being developed as a result of the fur trade and not because they were a long historical practice of those peoples (1935, 1937).

Jenness also went from histories of the past to the future. His book *The Indians of Canada* was the authoritative "handbook" on indigenous peoples of Canada for nearly half a century after its first edition appeared in 1932. It was divided into two parts: a thematic overview followed by a "tribal" survey. At the end of the first half of the book, Jenness wrote,

"Doubtless all the tribes will disappear" (1932: 264). Some will "merge steadily with the white race" while others, like the Inuit in the far north, may take centuries to fade away. But "culturally they have already contributed everything that was valuable for our own civilization" (1932: 264). The implications of Jenness's work for policy-makers differed significantly from those sought by Speck. Peter Kulchyski argues that, although Jenness was often critical of specific government policies, there was a "structural complicity between Jenness and the State" (1993: 38).

In response to Jenness's critiques and to others' criticisms of his claims that Algonquian hunting territories predated European contact, Speck developed and supplemented his claim for Algonquian aboriginality. Speck's initial claims for aboriginality were based partly on environmental determinist explanations, supplemented by distributional and historical arguments (e.g., 1926b, 1928). Critics of his position, who began publishing in 1916, cited mainly distributional and historical counter-evidence (Mechling, 1916a, 1916b; Strong, 1929; Jenness, 1932, 1935, 1937; Alfred G. Bailey, 1937, 1938, 1942; Julian Steward, 1936, 1938, 1941, 1955). Steward alone addressed himself to the environmental argument, saying that social and economic security required the unity of several families, that subdivided family hunting tracts would rarely provide sufficient varieties of foods, and that realignment, adjustments, and many practical difficulties were inherent in defined territories (1936: 332–33).

In the 1930s Speck, along with John M. Cooper, responded by developing the ecological-economic explanations of the hunting territory systems, first by casting it in an ecological possibilist framework. Speck came to recognize that not all of the most "primitive" of hunting peoples had systems of hunting territories, and in the boreal regions he distinguished between the northern zone of caribou hunters, where such a system was not found, and the more southerly zone, where it was (Speck, 1931). Cooper pointed out that certain groups adopted different systems, depending on whether they were hunting in one zone or the other, so that groups of hunters themselves did not necessarily use just one system on a permanent basis (Cooper, 1938: 58). Cooper, highlighting the distinction between tribal sovereignty and land tenure systems, claimed that everywhere in the east and north of North America "tribal lands" were recognized but that land tenure—that is, intratribal ownership—could be of several kinds (1938: 55).

A second change in the ecological arguments developed after the 1936 publication by Julian Steward of his essay "The Economic and Social Basis of Primitive Bands." In this essay, Steward discussed his methodology of focusing analyses on productive practices as the effective link between cultures and environments, as this could offer a cultural ecological explanation that was more comprehensive than environmental determinism or possibilism (Steward, 1936, as well as 1955).[5]

Speck and Loren C. Eiseley adopted Steward's method in their study of Algonquian territoriality and applied it to arguments in favour of the pre–fur trade development of hunting territories. Within the broad cultural history framework that Speck had used in much of his ethnographic analysis up to this time, the northeast of North America was a "marginal culture zone" characterized by an archaic culture and its stability (Fenton, 1991: 25, citing especially Speck, 1926b). The cultural ecology framework opened the way to a less tradition-based analysis.

The changes were clear in papers written by Speck and Eiseley (1939 and particularly 1942). In 1942 they argued that groups of hunters could be shown to use different systems of social and territorial organization not only when hunting in different zones but also within the same zone at different times. They argued this by reinterpreting the limited ethnographic records that had been assembled over the last three decades in the light of Steward's focus on productive activities. A single group could be organized as communal nomads or as sedentary families in either subarctic biogeographical zones—the tundra with caribou and fish or the coniferous forests with moose and small game, such as beaver. The differing social and territorial organizations were adopted by a group as changes in the abundance or scarcity of various animal populations changed their productive focus and harvesting activities (Speck and Eiseley, 1942: 220).

They thus added to Steward's cultural ecology the notion that the changing abundance or scarcity of resources relative to needs was an important variable (possibly drawing from Herskovits, 1940). This had the effect of responding to Steward's ecological arguments against hunting territories on the basis of the difficulties of adjusting the game harvests to family needs. Speck and Eiseley argued that the adjustments that were made included the periodic adoption or abandonment of hunting territory tenure as needed, and so social arrangements changed accordingly.

Speck abandoned the arguments based on the continuity of tenure arrangements in favour of a more dynamic model of adaptive choices in which hunting territories were but one of the options. This was also a more dynamic version of Steward's model that was not explicitly taken up by Steward.

Using these analytical frameworks, and the quite limited ethnographic evidence that was available, Speck and Eiseley reconstructed a hypothetical historical model of how systems of territoriality might have developed in response to changing productive conditions before the beginning of the fur trade. They argued that as bands penetrated new land, the land was considered a free good. If game became scarcer relative to human needs, a group consciousness of those living in the area would develop, just as continuity of residence developed and as a system of annually allotting lands among band members might have developed. From this form, hunting territories proper may have developed where husbanding of small game such as beaver was of value (Speck and Eiseley, 1942: 238–41). They summarized this in a diagram entitled "Chart Showing Possible Modes of Development of Both Band and Family Types of Ownership of Hunting Territories among the Algonkians of the Northeast" (1942: 237).

As Speck and Eiseley noted, this way of viewing hunting territories certainly does "not encourage its treatment as a static element of culture" (Speck and Eiseley, 1942: 241). In this explanation, social organization and tenure practices responded to variations in resource use which themselves responded to changes in resource abundances and human population sizes. Given these dynamics, they went on to argue that individual groups may have changed from one phase to another "and back again through the vagaries of historic chance" (1942: 241).

This model indicates that by 1942 Speck and Eiseley were giving historical priority not to forms of private property but to free access to lands, which could lead to communal forms of tenure, which in turn could lead to forms that they considered privatized. But they still held that private property could develop independently of trade and market production, and that Marxist models of social evolution were wrong. Thus, any claim that private property could only arise in the context of involvement of production for markets was denied.

The sequence was also reversible, given the cycles of animal abundance and the shifts in human population dynamics. Thus, evolutionary claims of a specific sequence or direction to the changes and variations that occurred, such as those of Steward, were also denied.

Speck and Eiseley offered an ecological and historical rather than an evolutionary model (see Deschênes, 1981: 212). Their model of changes that were not unidirectional was a significant break with Steward's quest for "cultural law[s]" (Steward, 1936: 331). It was also a challenge to those who asserted the evolutionary superiority of "Western" forms of using and conserving lands and resources, such as Vaux espoused.

Speck and Eiseley portrayed Algonquians as active and adaptive agents in both environmental and social history. This is reflected in

Speck's earlier report of Ojibwa arguments against the colonization of their lands (see his 1915 publications), and in his call for active indigenous involvement in government policy-making, which can be seen in his 1926 reply to Vaux, cited above. That being said, this was a largely formulaic and limited account of their agency in history, and it was more schematic than richly substantiated. Nevertheless, it is surprising that Speck and Eiseley's arguments have received little consideration in the subsequent critical analyses and histories of the Algonquian hunting territory debates.

Leacock on Colonialism, Acculturation, and Agency

The most influential account of the development of the Algonquian family hunting territory system as a result of the fur trade with Europeans, and not as a pre-contact productive adaptation, was offered by Eleanor Leacock in 1954. Leacock's arguments have been widely cited, and I recount them here only in part. Leacock made arguments about both pre– and post–fur trade Algonquian society, which I sometimes call pre- or post-contact.

Her specific claims about pre-contact Algonquians were based on the ethno-historical records from the post-contact seventeenth-century missionaries, records which predated the fur trade documents that Speck used (1954: 11) but which did not predate the fur trade. These records, Leacock claims, give "a clear picture of the simple fluid socioeconomic organization which is so characteristic of other hunting and gathering peoples ... and which is completely incompatible with the existence of the hunting-ground system as we know it" (Leacock 1954: 14).

René Gadacz has noted that the fur trade may already have led to changes in the indigenous peoples' way of life by the time of the missionary records of the first half of the seventeenth century (1975: 161). I have argued that the earlier post-contact evidence also suggests that pre–fur trade Montagnais society was not at all simple, although fluidity may be inferred from the records (Feit, 1994).

Leacock's image of pre–fur trade Algonquian social organization as simple and fluid seems idealized and uncomplicated in the light of the earlier fur trade records, some of which Leacock did cite (see 1954: 14). The records that are now available imply much more complexity. They indicate that in the first few years of the seventeenth century, Montagnais were middlemen in the fur trade, defending access to the European ships at Tadoussac against other bands. The records also indicate that they had established a trading network that extended many hundreds of miles from their points of trade; had formed alliances with some neighbouring groups in order to drive the Iroquois out of the St. Lawrence Valley; and had assembled over a thousand people at the trading harbour at Tadoussac at the time of Champlain's visit in 1603 (Bailey, 1937; Trigger, 1976; and Feit, 1994: 432, where the data are reviewed). These patterns are not consistent with the simple band societies that Leacock reads from later missionary records and that she takes as the model of pre–fur trade Montagnais societies. These records also remind us that the Jesuit images of Algonquians were European constructions made for European consumption.

Leacock's models of pre–fur trade Montagnais society were consistent with her readings of Marxist-socialist models. and specifically with primitive communism as the earliest stage of social evolution. She offered an analysis, and a condemnation, of the effects of the fur trade on indigenous societies. Her analysis of post–fur trade developments complimented her claim that private property did not exist before the fur trade, but it also focused on the social and human effects of the fur trade. This was shaped both by the historical Marxist critiques of capitalism and her interest in primitive communism (1993 [1984]), as well as by the deteriorating condition of indigenous peoples at her fieldwork sites.[6] On Leacock's theoretical and political views and her specific interest in primitive communism, see her engaging autobiographical essay "Being an Anthropologist" (1993 [1984]: especially 15).

Leacock has described a very rich and detailed period of fieldwork she undertook with the Innu (then Montagnais) of the north shore of the St. Lawrence River over two summers. Yet she wrote her dissertation concisely, "sticking to the argument over the hunting territory," and producing a text she described later as "polemic and analytical," that was forty-three pages long with an additional twenty-five pages of notes (Leacock, 1993 [1984]: 16–18, 19). The account she offered of the effects of the fur trade was structured as a highly formal three-stage model of the transformations wrought by shifts from production for use to production for trade. It was both critical of the mid-twentieth-century problems of the Innu social economy (caused by the fur trade) and a statement of their social evolution.

Leacock argued that formerly, "owing to uncertainties of the hunt, several families were necessarily dependent upon each other," providing a subsistence security greater than individual families could attain (Leacock 1954: 7). It was the introduction of production for trade, through a series of three evolutionary stages, that transferred the individual's most important economic ties from within the band to without and, as a result, changed the objective relation between band members from cooperative to competitive. Through these stages, families become self-sufficient through increased dependence on storable, transportable, and individually acquired purchased food supplies (Leacock 1954: 7). In contrast to the pre–fur trade situation, material needs become theoretically limitless, and larger living groups were "not only superfluous in the struggle for existence but a positive hindrance to the personal acquisition of furs.... The family group begins to resent intrusions that threaten to limit its take of furs and develops a sense of proprietorship over a certain area, to which it returns year after year for the sake of greater efficiency" (Leacock 1954: 7).

Leacock claimed these developments had begun by the beginning of the eighteenth century when clear evidence appeared suggesting there were individual family hunting and trapping arrangements in some areas (1954: 15). The process was essentially completed by 1950 at Seven Islands, Quebec, where she did some of her fieldwork (1954: 24). In western Quebec among the Innu at Lake St. John and the neighbouring Cree of Mistassini (1954: 36), based on the mid-1930s reports of Julius Lips, there were hunting territories but the process was not completed and hunting practices remained fluid (1954: 40). As well, among other Innu groups east of Seven Islands, where she also did fieldwork, the process was not completed (1954: 24, 27, 29). Thus, the current distribution of the family hunting territory practices showed that the "strength of individualized land-holding patterns characteristic of the western Montagnais decrease[d] ... *outward from the center of the earliest and most intensive fur trade*" and hunting territories were less developed within the region both to the east and west of the earliest trading sites (1954: 6; italics in original).

Leacock clearly presented the loss of collective relations and social values that such a transformation involved. She noted that these developments were not smooth or easy, but met considerable resistance from the Algonquians who were reluctant to give up communal patterns (1954: 9). She also noted that there were limited data on these processes as they occurred over the long period of the fur trade (1954: 16). Nevertheless, she emphasized the importance of the transformations by saying that the significance of the changes lay "more properly in the sphere of acculturation than in that of primitive economics proper" (Leacock, 1954: 1).

"Acculturation" was a developing area of debate in the periods immediately before and after the Second World War. The term had come into more than casual use in the mid-1930s, and its definition was debated into the 1950s. It most commonly referred to general cultural changes that resulted from sustained "contact" between groups or individuals having different cultures. But there were some who used the term specifically to describe changes created through the use of force, broadly defined (Beals, 1953).

Leacock's account presented changes as inevitable, given the growing Innu dependence on production for market trade as opposed to use within kin networks. She wrote that in the final stage of acculturation, Algonquian trappers "differ[ed] from white trappers only in the carry-over of some material traits, including at times a slightly, but hardly significant, greater dependence on natural products and, more markedly, in the retention of attitudes and personal relationships more closely correlated with their past than their present way of life" (Leacock, 1954: 24).

Her study was compassionate, and it can be seen today as a major forerunner of the now widely recognized need to locate societies in the context of their wider political economic relations and histories. Nevertheless, her work was also very formal and somewhat formulaic. It highlighted the power of trade and market institutions and their capacity to transform other societies, and it mentioned resistance only in passing. It made no mention of the roles and effects of state institutions that had become active at the time of her fieldwork but that were not active during most of the fur trade period. Her model of formal stages of transformation contributed to her presentation of the inevitability of transformations, as did the lack of any active agency of the Innu beyond an unspecified resistance or a lag in culture change.

Leacock's study was widely, almost universally, accepted in anthropology over the two decades following its publication, and it was only in the 1970s, after extended field research by a new generation of scholars as noted above, that it became clear that contemporary hunting territories were not a form of private property and that, without denying the impacts and exploitation that were central to the fur trade, many indigenous societies had been much less uniformly acculturated and transformed than what was claimed in the model she offered. By the 1970s these researchers had not found that among the Mistissini or other Cree peoples there was widespread abandonment of subsistence production in favour of market food staples, a predominance or independence of nuclear families, comprehensive transformation of cooperative into competitive relations, the placing of value on theoretically limitless material acquisitiveness, or the idea that land was private property in a fully market sense, although significant changes had occurred and were ongoing due to more than the fur trade (see Tanner, 1979; Scott, 1979, 1986, 1988; Feit, 1978, 1982, 1991b).

But at the time, Leacock's monograph was widely read, accepted and important even though it appeared during a vigorous period of Cold War propaganda and anti-Marxism.[7] Its popularity exceeded its contribution to subarctic ethnography and to acculturationist and Marxist-socialist accounts of the transformation of band societies because it also echoed wider social debates of the period. Leacock's field research took place following the Second World War and her monograph was completed in 1954. I think her arguments about the effects of production for markets and private property on Innu societies can be read alongside wider social critiques of the period about whether decolonization and development were replacing or reproducing colonialism and whether socialism or capitalist development offered real opportunities for economic modernization or local control of socio-economic transformations, or independence.

These debates also gave impetus to wide claims over the benefits or dangers of market societies and of Western exploitation of the peoples and lands of the former colonies, now referred to as the "Third World." I suggest that her monograph echoed the connections being made in debates about the similarities between the societies of the Third World and the treatment and need for development of indigenous peoples within the settler states, what is now called the Fourth World. These debates also occurred in the context of postwar reviews of earlier "Indian" policies in the U.S. and Canada. I think this helps to explain the exceptionally wide interest in her monograph.

The most famous use of her research, made without full and appropriate acknowledgement, was undertaken by Robert Murphy and Julian Steward, who were working from very different theoretical and applied contexts.[8] In their highly influential comparative analysis of the impacts of market forces on two societies (in Labrador and Brazil), published as "Tappers and Trappers" (1956) in the journal *Economic Development and Change,* they summarized their staged model of acculturation in a generalized passage that echoed Leacock:

> *When the people of an unstratified native society barter wild products found in extensive distribution and obtained through individual effort, the structure of the native culture will be destroyed, and the final culmination will be a culture type characterized by individual families having delimited rights to marketable resources and linked to the larger nation through trading centers.* (Murphy and Stewart, 1956: 353; italics in original)

Steward and Murphy's model, like Leacock's, was of a unidirectional change. Even if Steward's other work stressed that changes were multi-evolutionary, his analyses showed that societies all underwent the same types of development. Although their analytical aims and commitments differed radically, neither Steward nor Leacock considered the possibility of the continuation of distinct moral, productive, and social economies in contemporary indigenous or hunting societies.

In her autobiographical essay, Leacock noted, with an honesty that was characteristic of her, that this issue was raised with her by Gene Weltfish, one of her teachers at Columbia at the time she completed her dissertation and monograph, in 1952 and 1954, respectively (see Leacock, 1993 [1984]: 13–14, 21, 29). Leacock wrote,

> I no longer remember her words, but her point was that to document the impact of colonization on a people, no matter how well intentioned, did them a disservice if one presented colonialism as a one-way process and ignored their active participation in their own history and bypassed their effect, in turn, on the history of Europe. (1993 [1984]: 13–14)[9]

Leacock did indicate that there was Innu resistance to the effects of the fur trade, but Weltfish's advice may have come too late to change her analytical argument more thoroughly. Later, looking back and writing a "current assessment" in 1984, Leacock described how this original work among the Innu fit into her later projects and interests, saying that she had "outlined some of the constraints and the structured alternatives available to a people in a changing situation" (Leacock, 1993 [1984]: 29).

SLOBODIN'S DIFFERENT HISTORIES: AGENCY, UNEXPECTED PASTS, AND FUTURES YET TO BE

Dick Slobodin did not set his study of Gwich'in history and social organization in opposition to that of his colleagues; he presented it as an extension of the work done by anthropologists working in the eastern subarctic, but it repeatedly addressed the issues in that literature in new ways.[10] He wrote that Peel River Gwich'in history had to be about the continuing presence of several "groupings larger than the family" (1962: 4), that it "did not begin with White contact," nor was it focused on processes of acculturation (1962: 3), that change was not unilineal (1962: 86), and that the Gwich'in had an active role in their past and their future (1962: 89). In each of these areas of analysis, Dick substantially advanced the study of histories of subarctic peoples, and of indigenous peoples more generally. It is also clear that he drew questions, insights, and inspiration from the dynamic possibilities opened up by Speck and Eiseley and the critiques of the fur trade developed by Leacock, and that he offered a committed form of analysis that in various ways echoed both Speck and Leacock.

The histories Dick wrote are not chronologies or models, although they are selective and structured. In addition to changing environmental resources, trade, and colonialism, they cover a wide and partly unusual assemblage of topics. He included histories of the changing ways of subsisting, living together, travelling, talking, trading furs, engaging outsiders (both indigenous and non-native), and understanding and sharing stories about what was happening and what could be done. The breadth of his approach clearly puzzled at least one reviewer at the time (Osgood, 1963: 994).

I would say that he included not only topics from the analytical literature but also those that would be likely to emerge from the interactions of an inquisitive and careful ethnographer who listened to the themes that a subarctic people might raise in teaching an outsider about their lives and history. I think that he was an ethnographer who presented that material respectfully in the course of organizing his own account.

Thus, his history has a "polyvocal" structure, which can be "read" as expressing its creation in a dialogue. It is not a Gwich'in history, nor is it a self-conscious effort to use Gwich'in structures of knowledge. Nevertheless, it reads as a story that not only quotes from but has also been affected by conversations and participation with indigenous peoples and the histories they recount. This was unusual in ethnographic writing at the time.

In one section of his monograph, Dick presented Gwich'in history by period, and in much greater detail and less schematically than previous historical work in the subarctic. He drew upon a wide variety of published first-person sources by traders, missionaries, and other non-natives, and extensively used Gwich'in accounts, which was unusual. He told a history of the motives and means that led to the specific ways that the region was penetrated by Euro-Americans, as well as of complex Gwich'in trajectories and purposes. He relished giving short character sketches of various personalities, as well as analyzing the growth of institutions and the complexity of changing Gwich'in activities and organization.

In a second set of chapters, Dick set out the extra-familial social groups that could be found in Peel River Gwich'in society, indicating five types of groups that were present in the nineteenth century and that existed during his field research and one other type that was extinct. Three types of groups were organized around seasonal productive activities, although they organized other activities as well. They varied in size from four to eight families in two of the cases, and from ten to thirty in the third. Two of these groups would form for a season, the other would be reactivated seasonally over many years and was territorial. The formation of these three groups was clearly and systematically structured by productive activities and the kinds, numbers, and distributions of the animals that were being hunted, trapped, or fished. There was also a more complex panoply of social arrangements related to productive activities than any of those recognized or reported by the authors cited above. Dick also made clear that the social groups were related to activities other than subsistence and the production of goods for trade. The fourth type of group was known as the local group. Made up of four to eight families, it functioned as a "miniature community" and was concerned with all aspects of living within a defined habitat or territory. It was the most durable of the groups. The fifth group was a band assembly, a recurring but briefly assembled grouping that could include fifty to seventy families for trading, ceremonials, and games. The assembly was under the leadership of an adult trader, a ceremonial "chief," or a leader of high status, who functioned principally in "foreign affairs." This group was territorial, and it was often talked about as a kinship grouping.

Identities were determined by an individual belonging to a family, a local group, or a band, and these identities continued even when the members were scattered (for summaries, see Slobodin, 1962: 73–80). There were at least two "community" groupings larger than families and three "territorial" units in the Gwich'in social organization.

Dick denied that Gwitch'in practices confirmed "that 'customary use [led] to the concept of ownership,'" and he said that property rights "as known in agricultural and urban societies, [were] foreign to the Kutchin social order" (Slobodin, 1962: 61, quoting Steward, 1955: 135). He thus offered a complete alternative to the conclusions of the debates that had gone on within eastern subarctic anthropology. He did so more than a decade before eastern subarctic ethnographers began to revise accounts of Algonquian social and territorial organization.

Dick then analyzed Gwitch'in social groups through history in order to explore how Peel River Gwich'in used and modified social groups under different conditions. In these accounts two sets of stories stand out, those of the gold rush in the adjacent Yukon Territory, and those of the changes that took place in the fur trade during the first half of the twentieth century.

The Yukon gold rush (also referred to as the Klondike gold rush), which began in 1897, had had a diverse impact on the Gwich'in. Dick noted that it was important for the Peel River region that gold seekers only passed through the country, and only a few did so at that, since it was not the main route to the Yukon gold fields (1962: 30). But contact with the gold rush did reorient the activities of the Peel River Gwitch'in people toward the southwest Yukon. By 1901 they were spending their summers in and around Dawson City, the centre of the gold rush (1962: 30–31). The major activity of the Peel River people in winter was hunting meat, which they supplied to the gold rush sites. As a result, they spent part of each winter in large "meat camps" of fifteen to twenty families, as they had done previously when caribou were abundant (1962: 31–32). In summer they worked in a range of occupations, many new to them, but many of which still involved work as fishers for the food market and as woodcutters for the fuel supply (1962: 32). Others took new and diverse forms of employment.

The contacts with other indigenous peoples, with whom the Peel River people camped near Dawson, also led to a revival of potlatching, which was associated with visiting the Yukon peoples and which had declined during the nineteenth century (1962: 33–34). Dick noted that in this region a "*sine qua non* of the potlatch was the presence of guests" (1962: 34). The social contacts with southwestern groups also tended to reinforce connections with siblings, the prerogatives of wealth-ranking, and the importance of community rituals and band assemblages.

But at the same time, the Gwich'in "gained intimate experience of Western Civilization in the rampantly individualistic and indeed anarchic form of a gold-rush and frontier boom" (1962: 81–82). However, the boom did not endure and by the middle of the First World War most Peel River people had returned to live on the Peel River, where the "regimen of the nineteenth century" was resumed, until circumstances again changed (1962: 34–35).

Dick noted that there were many "novelties in material goods and experience," and that the period had a variety of longer-term effects. Speaking of the late 1940s when he did his fieldwork, he noted that "there exists the paradoxical or at least unusual situation that many or most of the band elders have had experience of frontier culture unknown to younger men ... [for instance, the] 'Dawson Boys' speak [English] more fluently and more colloquially than do many of the younger members of the band" (1962: 33). The elders also had a "lively appreciation of the hazards of the frontier situation . . . [and the] demoralized state of their friends and relatives [around Dawson, which] ... was discussed at length at a band meeting in 1946, with the fervent conclusion that 'we must never let this happen to us'" (1962: 33; also see 1963).

After the First World War a different set of market-driven shifts affected resource-use patterns and social organization. Dick offered specifics on the changes in the "world fur market" and changing fur prices, as well as in regional and local conditions, including the changing structure and types of trade organizations and financing, the diverse fur-sales arrangements Peel River people used. These analyses are considerably more detailed than those cited by other anthropologists working in the subarctic at that time, both with respect to the nature of trade and markets and with respect to Gwitch'in productive activities.

Muskrat pelt production and trade on the lower reaches of the Peel River became an important spring hunt from the 1920s on because of rising fur prices. Muskrat hunting was done mostly by families or paired families, who shared a single household and who were spread out along the waterways. This pattern continued throughout the subsequent decades, but only seasonally.

Post–Second World War fur prices made marten also attractive and it was caught high in the mountains in winter. When Peel River families and men returned to using these areas after the war, Dick accompanied them (1962: 47–53). Their return to these areas was motivated by and dependent on high fur prices.

He found that this country retained "much symbolic value as the country *par excellence* of 'the real Indians'" (1962: 40). He noted that many "locations, objects, and activities which, downriver, are mentioned only in traditional tales are matters of immediate reference in mountain country" (1962: 40).

Trapping parties of four to eight families were formed and reformed, along with single and paired families. Different and specialized travel skills and knowledge were needed and taught by example, and Dick gave a graphic account of the effects of extreme cold on the people, their perceptions, and the equipment, from his own experience with a trapping party (1962: 49). He also noted, "I was chagrined to find that I was less able to follow conversations than I had been in the settlement" (1962: 40). A young Gwich'in commented to Dick, "When they get up here in the mountains, these people talk a different way, more like the old days" (1962: 40).

Some Peel River men used a system for selling their fine furs that started in the early 1930s. They shipped their most valuable furs directly to auction houses in western Canada and Seattle by air, receiving payment through Edmonton bank accounts, and ordering supplies for the next winter to be shipped by air freight during the summer by suppliers in southern

Canada. He noted that the marten trappers, because of high prices in the 1940s, "hoped to emancipate themselves from the local 'debt' trading system" (1962: 40).

He also noted, in his discussion of band or community leadership, that "second chiefs," whose positions were enhanced by fur traders and governments so that the incumbents could act as intermediaries, were not effective when asked to serve as minor traders. "If he had to choose between acting in terms of Euro-American commercial good faith and conforming to the standards of generosity and helpfulness expected of a leading man in the community, the latter expectation prevailed" (1962: 72). This showed the continuing strength of the values of generosity and help, and Dick notes that the two contemporary band councillors "oriented toward Euro-American standards of political and commercial success ... lowered their prestige" by their behaviour (1962: 72).

Here the effects of the fur trade and its relationship to acculturation, social groups, social sharing, and values are complex and variable, as are the strategies of the Gwich'in. This is a dramatically different story than that offered by Speck or Leacock. "Trapping for the Euro-American fur trade has certainly inaugurated a series of changes, still continuing, in Peel River culture, but ... [they] do not seem overwhelming" (Slobodin, 1962: 83).

Dick also pointed out, "Peel River social history to date has been characterized more by continuity, or by variations around long-established norms, than by drastic change" (1962: 84). He recognized that there were a series of "permissive" historical circumstances that facilitated these conditions, and he noted that the "conditions of culture contact during the last century or so ... permit[ted] the continued operation of what may be termed the principles of Peel River social organization" (1962: 84). He also noted that the effects of the historic changes were not "unidirectional" nor did the "opportunism and adaptability of the Peel River people to the variety of situations which has confronted" them imply that their "society [was] amorphous" (1962: 86–87). It is the continuity of structures, social and others, which he emphasized in the historical processes, along with the contingent conditions that might have been otherwise.

Dick stressed contingency as well as opportunity. He highlighted that had the past been different, the Gwich'in might have suffered much more dreadfully, and that they still might. He noted, "speculative[ly]," that had the early fur trade come into the Peel River region from the Yukon and not from the Mackenzie drainage, the Gwich'in would have been more permanently involved in the middle Yukon and it was "unlikely that the Peel

River people could have then escaped the cultural disruption and demor-
alization which have characterized middle Yukon communities since the
gold rush" (1962: 84).

Dick recognized a contingent but structured and structuring past, but
in doing so he did not predict the future. In the afterword, speaking about
the future, he noted, "One may wonder whether the dialectics of intensi-
fied culture contact will be as irrational, the results as anarchic, as in the
past colonial and frontier situations" (1962: 88). He went on to express
concerns about the future of the caribou, the environment, and the effects
of industry and of social welfare. He also wrote, "The hunting people we
discerned at the outset, grey-black in the Arctic winter, face new problems, new opportunities, and, eventually, the creation of new social forms"
(1962: 88).

CONCLUSION: GWICH'IN DIALOGUES WITH SLOBODIN ON VISIONS AND HISTORIES OF THE FUTURE

Dick said in his introduction that the "history of the Peel River Kutchin
in recent generations has not been that of a people who 'helplessly accept
the conqueror's ways, or passively die out, or go down fighting with a
spear or the gun,' nor yet has there been a 'moral regeneration' in a nativistic movement" (1962: 5). This passage as well as the closing paragraphs
of his monograph are set in a wider context of ideas and critiques of that
period.

The quotes in Dick's text cited in the paragraph above come from
Robert Redfield's chapter "Civilization and the Moral Order" in *The Primitive World and Its Transformations* (1957). Redfield's book fits the
post–Second World War rethinking of the place of the "West" in a changing world in need of development and moral leadership.

Redfield said that world religions "may be recognized as the first great
expansions of moral order to transcend the local community and the local
culture and to embrace all humanity" (1957: 80). He continued, "the
immense creativeness they represent was made possible by the expansive
and disintegrative nature of civilization itself," noting that the "anthropologist encounters this creativity of the disintegrated folk society in the form
of nativistic movements. The impact of civilization upon the primitive
societies results in part in the stimulation of new ideas, new religions, and
ethical concepts" (Redfield, 1957: 80). Redfield then went on to the passage that Slobodin quoted directly, that "not all primitive peoples helplessly
accept the conqueror's ways," but among those who do not "there are

many cases of moral regeneration" (Redfield, 1957: 80). Dick Slobodin commented that "these types of eventuality have been of great concern to the anthropologist" (1962: 5).

It was this idea that primitive societies need and will necessarily undergo regeneration, and that this renewal and development comes from contacts with the ideas of civilized societies and civilization that Dick Slobodin rejected, in part based on his experiences with the Gwich'in and their histories (Slobodin, 1962: 5). He said of his study that "it is felt that a distinctive contribution may be made from the study of a people who actively maintain a hunting economy, who display considerable *esprit de corps,* and whose social forms show at once the mark of tradition and a capacity for adaptation to current situations" (1962: 5).

Ten years later he returned to the topic, saying that an "assumption underlying human research and administrative policy concerning the American North is that homogenisation and the obliteration of communal or regional cultural differences will continue until a kind of dead anomic uniformity prevails" (1975: 287). He noted that "a few observers have ventured to question whether this 'deculturization' must continue to its logical conclusion throughout the 'developing' world,'" and he cited the "French Marxist sociologist" Henri Lefebvre whose views could challenge the assumptions articulated by Redfield. Lefebvre asked if "after a period of crisis, cultural diversification ... will not reemerge" (Slobodin, 1975: 287).

Redfield's argument went on to locate the moral transformations he envisaged in "the primitive world" in the emergence of universal ideas in history (Redfield, 1957: 80–83). These ideas both fit into the enduring tradition of the European Enlightenment and the post–Second World War establishment of a renewed international system, best symbolized by the United Nations, the promise of global development, and the recognition of human rights. Redfield went on to say that while some see these as bold ideas and others see them as unrealistic, nevertheless "they are among the movers and shakers of human affairs" (1957: 83). In concluding his chapter, Redfield noted that these "great ideas in history are possible only in civilization. The precivilized and the isolated preliterate are unaffected by them" (Redfield, 1957: 83).

Dick tells a different story, and this is highlighted in the penultimate paragraph of his book. It is different in part because it shifts the focus to another "great idea" that Westerners tell to non-Western peoples as well as themselves, about individualism and success. It is also different in shifting the viewpoint to someone speaking from a hunting and gathering society. Dick quotes a Peel River man who told him:

"White men are trying to teach us things it looks like a lot of you people don't believe any more." The speaker was not referring to the contrast between the precept of missionaries and the practice of many White men; the natives have long taken this discrepancy for granted. He was remarking, rather, upon our culture's entrepreneurial folklore of individual, self-regarding effort as the key to success. "Every man for himself—I see lots of white men don't think so. For us, we got to stick together, that's our way," he added. (Slobodin, 1962: 89)

Dick's presentation of this story reveals a Gwich'in commentary on the tales being told to them by white men about how they should change and what the future holds for them. It reveals how they are not convinced by the future that whites portray, or even that the whites generally hold this vision with full conviction any more. This commentary not only questions the white stories of the history of the future but affirms that Gwich'in are living and seeking their own histories and future.

In contrast to the numerous government officials, anthropologists, and other non-natives who see the past and future as part of progressive change, Dick questions the assumptions of general historical progress, past and future. He did not do this to deny differences, to reject structures, or to obviate evaluative work, all of which he consistently engaged in. He did it to recreate recognition of indigenous and, more generally, collective agency.

The unknown but not limitless possibilities for the future, and the plurality of contested histories of the future, are emphasized here. I think they are quietly expressed in the Gwitch'in commentary he cited near the end of his book. The Peel River man seems to, unexpectedly, not only reject and query the power of whites' visions of history and the future, but he also seems to open the possibility that whites who do not believe their own history of the future might come to share with Gwich'in some other stories and future.

NOTES

1   I have been stimulated to develop this paper in this form by the comments made at the Symposium in Honour of Richard Slobodin held at the Canadian Anthropology Society meetings at Concordia University, Montreal, on May 12, 2006, and especially the comments offered there and afterwards by Tony Fisher, Sam Ajzenstat, Michael Asch, and Dick Preston. I want to thank the many Waswanipi hunters who took the time and effort over the years to teach me something about what they know and how they envision their past and their futures. The research on which this paper is based was done with the assistance of research grants from the Social Sciences and Humanities Research Council of Canada (SSHRC), and from the McMaster University Arts Research Board.

2 I will use the current spelling of "Algonquian" except in quoted passages and "Gwich'in" except in quoted passages.

3 I have used the terms "indigenous" or "indigenous people" for First Nations (Canadian usage) and Native Americans (U.S. usage), although I retain "Indian" where the reference is to non-indigenous institutions or ideas.

4 This assessment is based on oral comments made by several speakers and questioners at a seminar on Speck at the annual meetings of the American Anthropological Association in Philadelphia, in 1986. Some of the presentations were subsequently edited and published in Blakenship (1991). One relatively early written record of Speck's frustration and his cynicism and implied criticism was his terse refusal to accept an invitation from the Canadian minister of justice to provide information relating to the indigenous peoples of the Labrador interior for the mammoth legal case *Re Labrador Boundary*, an intergovernmental dispute over the boundary between the Dominion of Canada and the then British colony of Newfoundland, which worked its way up to the British Privy Council. Speck replied to the request in 1922 briefly, saying, "I regret ... to have to say that my own studies are so far from complete though I have been at work on them since 1904" (Speck, [1922]). Speck seemed more comfortable as the critic and maverick than as an acknowledged adviser and expert to governments.

5 For an assessment of how Steward argued throughout his career against the possibility of private property and any Indigenous legal rights in band hunting and gathering societies, see Pinkowski and Asch (2004). These authors also show how Steward's views were expressed both in his theoretical models and in his applied work as an expert witness for government, and how his views have affected legal rulings quite widely, and continue to do so.

6 That her 1954 monograph cites only ethno-historic and ethnographic sources (such as Speck, Cooper, Steward, Jenness, Bailey, Lips, and Strong) but not authors whose work primarily focused on debates about Marxist–socialist models (such as Engels, Morgan, Lowie, and Mechling), reflects the political constraints of the period. Leacock notes in her autobiographical essay that at her pre-dissertation oral examination some years earlier, "as always, I answered everything fully, empirically, while keeping my Marxist 'neo-evolutionary' views to myself" (1993 [1984]: 14). This reflects both general conditions and her personal experience. After completing her B.A. from Barnard College in 1944, and before she entered graduate school, Leacock was denied clearance by the FBI to work with Ruth Benedict and Rhoda Metreaux on their wartime analysis of cultural themes in a project developed under the Office of War Information and the Office of Strategic Services in Washington (1993 [1984]: 11).

7 Lee and Daley also ask why Leacock's formulation was so influential, given the challenges it faced (1993: 36).

8 On her relationship with and treatment by Steward, see Leacock's own comments (1993 [1984]: 19–21).

9 Weltfish was an important influence on Leacock while she was a graduate student at Columbia (1993 [1984]: 12–14). Leacock noted that she "took her comment most seriously" (1993 [1984]: 13).

10 This collaborative approach was clearly a related to Dick's particularly colle-
gial style of scholarship and dialogue. Dick, who received his Ph.D. from
Columbia, knew personally many of those who had published on the topic.
Steward had been on the faculty at Columbia from 1946 to 1952 (Murphy,
1977). Murphy was a graduate student there during that period (Murphy,
1977) and later a faculty member. Leacock did her Ph.D. there and appears to
have been there from around the end of the Second World War to the mid-1950s
(Leacock, 1993 [1984]). She gives an account of some of the tensions and conflicts that developed, particularly those with Steward. Among an earlier generation, W.D. Strong, whose fieldwork findings challenged Speck's early views
on the wide distribution of hunting territories, was still there during the periods when both Slobodin and Leacock attended.

REFERENCES

Bailey, Alfred G. 1937. *The Conflict of European and Eastern Algonkian Cultures,
1504–1700. A Study in Canadian Civilization*. Fredericton: New Brunswick
Museum Publications, Monograph Series, No. 2.
———. 1938. "Social Revolution in Eastern Canada." *Canadian Historical Review*
19(3): 264–76.
———. 1942. "The Indian Problem in Early Canada." *America Indigena* 2(3):
35–39.
Beals, Ralph. 1953. "Acculturation." In A.L. Kroeber, ed., *Anthropology Today*,
621–41. Chicago: University of Chicago Press.
Blakenship, Roy, ed. 1991. *The Life and Times of Frank G. Speck, 1881–1950*.
Publications in Anthropology, No. 4. Philadelphia: University of Pennsyl-
vania.
Cooper, John M. [1933]. "Aboriginal Land Holding Systems." Memorandum to
Dr. Harold W. McGill, Deputy Superintendent General for Indian Affairs,
Ottawa, Canada. October 11. 13 typescript pages plus map.
———. 1938. "Land Tenure among the Indians of Eastern and Northern North
America." *Pennsylvania Archaeologist* 8: 55–60.
———. 1939. "Is the Algonquian Family Hunting Ground System Pre-Columbian?"
American Anthropologist 41: 66–90.
Deschenes, Jean-Guy. 1981. "La contribution de Frank G. Speck à l'anthropolo-
gie des Amérindiens du Quebec." *Recherches amérindiennes au Québec*
9(3): 205–20.
Engels, Frederick. 1972 [1884]. *The Origin of the Family, Private Property and
the State*. Introduction and Notes by Eleanor Burke Leacock. New York:
International Publishers.
Feit, Harvey A. 1978. "Waswanipi Realities and Adaptations." Ph.D. dissertation.
McGill University.
———. 1982. "The Future of Hunters within Nation States: Anthropology and
the James Bay Cree." In Eleanor B. Leacock and Richard B. Lee, eds., *Politics and History in Band Societies*, 373–411. Cambridge: Cambridge University Press.

———. 1991a. "The Construction of Algonquian Hunting Territories: Private Property as Moral Lesson, Policy Advocacy and Ethnographic Error." In George W. Stocking Jr., ed., *Colonial Situations*, 109–34. Madison: University of Wisconsin Press.

———. 1991b. "Gifts of the Land: Hunting Territories, Guaranteed Incomes and the Construction of Social Relations in James Bay Cree Society." *Senri Ethnological Studies* (Osaka) 30: 223–68.

———. 1994. "The Enduring Pursuit: Land, Time, and Social Relationships in Anthropological Models of Hunter-Gatherers and in Hunters' Images." In Ernest S. Burch, Jr., and Linda J. Ellanna, eds., *Key Issues in Hunter-Gatherer Research*, 421–39. Oxford: Berg Publishers.

———. 2004. "Les territoires de chasse algonquiens avant leur 'découverte'? Études et histoires sur la tenure, les incendies de forêt et la sociabilité de la chasse." *Recherches amérindiennes au Québec* 34(3): 5–21.

———. 2005. "Re-Cognizing Co-Management as Co-Governance: Histories and Visions of Conservation at James Bay." *Anthropologica* 47(2): 267–88.

———. N.d.a. "Algonquian Hunting Territories before Contact." Unpublished manuscript.

———. N.d.b. "Hunting Territories: A History of the Debates." Unpublished manuscript.

Fenton, William N. 1991. "Frank G. Speck's Anthropology (1881–1950)." In Roy Blakenship, ed., *The Life and Times of Frank G. Speck, 1881–1950*, 9–37. Publications in Anthropology, No. 4. Philadelphia: University of Pennsylvania.

Gadacz, René. 1975. "Montagnais Hunting Dynamics in Historico-ecological Perspective." *Anthropologica* 17(2): 149–69.

Hallowell, A. Irving. 1949. "The Size of Algonkian Hunting Territories: A Function of Ecological Adjustment." *American Anthropologist* 51(1): 35–45.

———. 1951. "Frank Gouldsmith Speck, 1881–1950." *American Anthropologist* 53: 67–75.

Hays, Samuel P. 1969 [1959]. *Conservation and the Gospel of Efficiency: The Progressive Conservation Movement, 1890–1920*. New York: Atheneum.

Herskovits, M.J. 1940. *The Economic Life of Primitive Peoples*. New York: Alfred A. Knopf.

Hoxie, Frederick E. 1984. *A Final Promise: The Campaign to Assimilate the Indians, 1880–1920*. Lincoln: University of Nebraska Press.

Jenness, Diamond. 1932. *The Indians of Canada*. Ottawa: National Museum of Canada, Bulletin No. 65.

———. 1935. *The Ojibwa Indians of Parry Island*. Ottawa: National Museum of Canada, Bulletin No. 78.

———. 1937. *The Sekani Indians of British Columbia*. Ottawa: National Museum of Canada, Bulletin No. 84.

Kulchyski, Peter. 1993. "Anthropology in the Service of the State: Diamond Jenness and Canadian Indian Policy." *Journal of Canadian Studies* 28(2): 21–40.

Leacock, Eleanor. 1954. *The Montagnais Hunting Territory and the Fur Trade*. Memoir 78. Washington, DC: American Anthropological Association.

————. 1993 [1984]. "Being an Anthropologist." In Constance R. Sutton, ed., *From Labrador to Samoa*, 1–31. Washington, DC: Association for Feminist Anthropology, American Anthropological Association.

Lee, Richard B., and Richard H. Daly. 1993. "Eleanor Leacock, Labrador, and the Politics of Gatherer-Hunters." In Constance R. Sutton, ed., *From Labrador to Samoa*, 33–46. Washington, DC: Association for Feminist Anthropology, American Anthropological Association.

Lips, Julius. 1947. *Naskapi Law: Transactions of the American Philosophical Society*. Vol. 37, No. 4.

Lowie, Robert H. 1920. *Primitive Society*. New York: Boni and Liveright.

Mechling, W.H. 1916a. "Review of Speck, *Family Hunting Territories and Social Life of Various Algonkian Bands of the Ottawa Valley*." *American Anthropologist* 18: 281–82.

————. 1916b. "Dr. Speck's 'The Family Hunting Band.'" *American Anthropologist* 18: 299–302.

Morgan, Lewis Henry. 1963 [1877]. In Eleanor Burke Leacock, ed., *Ancient Society*. Cleveland: World Publishing Company.

Murphy, Robert F. 1977. "Introduction." In Jane C. Steward and Robert F. Murphy, eds., *Evolution and Ecology*, 1–39. Urbana: University of Illinois Press.

Murphy, Robert F., and Julian H. Steward. 1956. "Tappers and Trappers: Parallel Processes in Acculturation." *Economic Development and Culture Change* 4: 335–55.

Osgood, Cornelius. 1963. "Review of *Band Organization of the Peel River Kutchin*." *American Anthropologist* 65: 944.

Pinchot, Gifford. [1919]. "The Use of the Natural Resources by the Indians." Talk presented at the University of Pennsylvania Houston Club. In Pinchot Papers, Library of Congress, Manuscripts Division.

Pinkoski, Marc, and Michael Asch. 2004. "Anthropology and Indigenous Rights in Canada and the United States: Implications in Steward's Theoretical Project." In Alan Barnard, ed., *Hunter-Gatherers in History, Archaeology, and Anthropology*, 187–200. Oxford: Berg.

Price, David H. 2004. *Threatening Anthropology: McCarthyism and the FBI's Surveillance of Activist Anthropologists*. Durham, NC: Duke University Press.

Pulla, Siomonn P. 2003. "Frank Speck and the Moise River Incident: Anthropological Advocacy and the Question of Aboriginal Fishing Rights in Quebec." *Anthropologica* 45: 129–45.

Redfield, Robert. 1957. *The Primitive World and Its Transformations*. Ithaca, NY: Cornell University Press.

Scott, Colin H. 1979. *Modes of Production and Guaranteed Annual Income in James Bay Cree Society*. Montreal: McGill University Programme in the Anthropology of Development.

————. 1986. "Hunting Territories, Hunting Bosses and Communal Production among Coastal James Bay Crees." *Anthropologica* 28(1–2): 163–73.

————. 1988. "Property, Practice and Aboriginal Rights Among Quebec Cree Hunters." In Tim Ingold, David Riches, and James Woodburn, eds., *Hunters and Gatherers*, Vol. 2: *Property, Power and Ideology*, 35–51. New York: Berg.

Slobodin, Richard. 1962. *Band Organization of the Peel River Kutchin*. National Museum of Canada Bulletin No. 179. Ottawa: Northern Affairs and National Resources.

———. 1963. "'The Dawson Boys': Peel River Indians and the Klondike Gold Rush." *Polar Notes* 5: 24–36.

———. 1969. "Leadership and Participation in a Kutchin Trapping Party." In David Damas, ed., *Contributions to Anthropology: Band Societies*, 56–89. Ottawa: National Museum of Canada, Bulletin No. 228.

———. 1975. "Canadian Subarctic Athapaskans in the Literature to 1965." *Canadian Review of Sociology and Anthropology* 12(3): 278–89.

Speck, Frank G. 1912. "Conservation for the Indians." *The Southern Workman* 41(6): 328–32.

———. 1913. "Conserving and Developing the Good in the Indian." *The Red Man* 5(10): 463–65.

———. 1914. "The Basis of Indian Ownership of Land and Game." *The Southern Workman* 43(1): 35–38.

———. 1915a. "Basis of American Indian Ownership of the Land." *University of Pennsylvania, University Lectures Delivered by Members of the Faculty in the Free Public Lecture Course 1914–1915*, 181–96. Pamphlet "reprint from Old Penn."

———. 1915b. *Family Hunting Territories and Social Life of Various Algonkian Bands of the Ottawa Valley*. Memoir 70. Ottawa: Geological Survey.

———. 1915c. "The Family Hunting Band ss the Basis of Algonkian Social Organization." *American Anthropologist* 17(2): 289–305.

———. 1922. Letter to E.L. Newcombe, Deputy Minister of Justice, Canada. Speck Papers, American Philosophical Society, Box 25.

———. 1926a. "Annihilating the Indian." *The General Magazine and Historical Chronicle* 28: 262–70.

———. 1926b. "Culture Problems in Northeastern North America." *Proceedings, American Philosophical Society* 65: 272–311.

———. 1928. "Land Ownership among Hunting Peoples in Primitive America and the World's Marginal Areas." *Proceedings 22nd International Congress of Americanists*, Vol. 2, 323–32. Rome.

———. 1931. "Montagnais Bands and Early Eskimo Distribution in the Labrador Peninsula." *American Anthropologist* 33(4): 557–600.

———. 1936. "Eskimo and Indian Backgrounds in Southern Labrador (Part 2)." *General Magazine and Historical Chronicle* 38: 143–63.

Speck, Frank G., and Loren C. Eiseley. 1939. "The Significance of Hunting Territory Systems of the Algonkian in Social Theory." *American Anthropologist* 41(2): 269–80.

———. 1942. "Montagnais–Naskapi Bands and Family Hunting Districts of Central and Southeastern Labrador Peninsula." *Proceedings, American Philosophical Society* 85(2): 215–42.

Steward, Julian H. 1936. "The Economic and Social Basis of Primitive Bands." In Robert Lowie, ed., *Essays in Anthropology Presented to A.L. Kroeber*, 331–45. Berkeley: University of California Press.

———. 1938. *Basin-Plateau Sociopolitical Groups*. Bulletin No. 120. Washington, DC: Bureau of American Ethnology.

———. 1941. "Determinism in Primitive Society?" *Scientific Monthly* 53(6): 491–501.

———. 1955. *Theory of Culture Change*. Urbana: University of Illinois Press.

Strong, W. Duncan. 1929. "Cross-cousin Marriage and the Culture of the Northeastern Algonkian." *American Anthropologist* 31(2): 277–88.

Tanner, Adrian. 1979. *Bringing Home Animals*. St. John's, NF: Memorial University Institute of Social and Economic Research.

Trigger, Bruce. 1976. *The Children of Aataenstsic. A History of the Huron People to 1660*. 2 Vols. Montreal: McGill-Queen's University Press.

Vaux, George. 1926. "Some Activities of the Federal Indian Bureau." *The General Magazine and Historical Chronicle* 28: 100–106.

CHAPTER SIX

Slobodin "among the Metis," 1938–98: Anthropologist, Scholar, Historian, and Fieldworker *par excellence*

Mary Black-Rogers

I chose to honour Richard Slobodin with a look back at our last century's ways and means for anthropologists to learn about "alien cultures." In particular, when the subject population consists of "persons possessing [a] ... 'mixed' racial and cultural heritage." That is how the preface reads in Slobodin's multi-dimensional report titled *Metis of the Mackenzie District* (1966), which I will describe as I encountered it for the first time and then started tracing its travels through the remaining decades of that century. This publication was fundamentally a report to the Canadian government[1] that managed to incorporate a number of anthropology's "aspects of culture" and the required personal experience in the field (the word "among" used to signal the last). It was not quite, I will propose, a "comprehensive ethnographic account" (see Ed Rogers's review, below), nor was it intended to be, although the author himself used the word "ethnography" on occasion (and used "among" twice, on page 56), while also pointing out the difficulties in dealing with "'mixed' populations," as he titled his first chapter, and with "Metis identity," as he titled his last. He described then tackled these problems, trying out and providing some solutions. After all, the task of "identifying" the residents of the district about whom the government wished to be informed would have to be the first consideration—whether for ethnography or for government. The manner in which this book delved into both, while at the same time keeping them separate, is discussed below.

In the decades that followed, this contribution continued to be a primary reference. It was cited for its "scholarly focus on metis culture and identity" (Peterson and Brown 1985: 6) and, late in the century, as a rich source of data for the project that led to the publication of "Metis History in the Mackenzie Basin" (1998); for these, see below.

At the boundaries of recognized areas of scholarly studies, Dick Slobodin could be counted on to let the tail of the thing wag him and his inquisitive mind as far as he wished it to do so. His scholarship was far-reaching and his interests deep. Yet he rarely drew "final conclusions," no matter how deeply he had pursued a subject; rather, he left the matter open to discussion and argument.

PERSONAL MEMORIES

A short personal note first—and a "story" (in keeping with the reputed Slobodin way).[2] I did not know Richard Slobodin very well, or long, personally. When I met him he was a colleague at McMaster University of my husband, Ed Rogers, who had a cross-appointment from the ROM's ethnology department one day a week. When my husband passed away, in 1988, Dick was one of the speakers at the memorial service.[3] During my remaining decade in Ontario, I enjoyed Dick's company, and that of his household, on several occasions. When I heard he had passed away, my reaction was quickly and clearly at hand: I recalled a gentle man, kind and quietly perceptive. Then a picture flashed from memory—he was as well a gentle Man of Action! And here's the "story":

> What flashed through my memory was a scene on the night of my mother's eighty-eighth birthday. An occasion during which he had suddenly appeared beside me, surfacing out of the partying crowd at our house and offering to help me drive my mother home. (The party had been for Mother's birthday; she had thrilled to the attention while it lasted—now was the moment to slip her out.) My relief was great, but I was concerned and said, "You'd have to wait while I help her to bed." To which he responded, "Fine, there's a radio program I'd like to hear in the car."
>
> No one else in the crowd had noticed. I thoroughly enjoyed that dreaded ride, on the icy streets, and up the steep icy driveway to where my mother was staying. I can even believe that Dick enjoyed the radio program while waiting in his car. I have no memory at all of what we spoke about otherwise. Not about the subarctic, I feel sure.

But what could I contribute to a session in his honour? With his work, as with the man personally, I had small acquaintance. My work had been deeply embedded in the Shield subarctic area east of Lake Winnipeg to

Hudson Bay (and, earlier, in northern Minnesota). The far northwest I had yet to discover. Then I spied a title on the section of my bookshelf that is devoted to personal ongoing research. The book was called *Metis of the Mackenzie District*, by Richard Slobodin (1966). I knew I could say something about that. Ed and I had allowed each other one day a week, during our semi-annual visits to the fur trade archives, to spend time researching personal interests apart from our joint work.[4] On those "free" days at the archives, I could usually be found in the area of Great Slave Lake and north (checking on my ancestors, where the Metis line began. I did not know then that it was also Slobodin land).

The book by Slobodin on the shelf must have belonged to Ed—it looked considerably worn—which was later confirmed when I came across his review of it, which began, "This is the first comprehensive ethnographic account of the Metis to be published" (Rogers, 1967). Relevant portions of his review are cited below.

Dick Slobodin's North, from His Preface

The title page of his book describes his work as a government report "in fulfillment of a contract October 1, 1962, through March 31, 1964, with the Research Centre, Department of Northern Affairs and Natural Resources." In his preface, he introduces us to Dick Slobodin, the person, in his North and in his youth:

> In the Fall of 1938, I found myself preparing to winter at a settlement in the Mackenzie District, Northwest Territories. I was told that a local resident had a vacant cabin which he might be willing to rent. This man was a "halfbreed"; one of his grandparents had been Indian, the other three Scottish. Newly arrived at the settlement and inexperienced in the ways of the North, I went to see the man in anticipation of a difficult session with a wily Metis.
>
> A first impression did not relieve my misgivings. There was a sardonic glint in his eye and a slight smile that to my apprehensive mind suggested a tough and tricky operator.
>
> He proposed ten dollars a month as rent.
>
> "I don't think I can afford that. How about ...," I ventured, "let's say, seven-fifty?"
>
> His smile widened slightly. "We don't like odd sums down here. Make it five dollars."

So the bargain was struck. The "halfbreed" became my land-lord; in time, a good friend; and, through the years, a valued source and advisor in ethnographic work....

The implications of this anecdote may serve to introduce a study of the Mackenzie District Metis.... I was not unusually burdened with prejudice. I was prepared to like and to respect Indians and Eskimos. When it came to "halfbreeds," however, I was under the sway of stereotypes about irresponsible misfits, inheriting the worst attributes of their ancestral races. This stereotype was shattered during that first winter in the North.

... In many human societies, although not in all, [those persons] ... possessing ... "mixed" racial and cultural heritage must cope with rather severe prejudice. In no society does this appear to be more true than in that of English-speaking North America. Members of the dominant majority may hold in scant regard the partially-urbanized Indians and Eskimos;... nevertheless they have an idealized image of the "old time," the "real" and "unspoiled" Indian and Eskimo. In this popular view, however, there never has been an "unspoiled halfbreed"; the very phrase is a contradiction in terms. (ix–x)

SLOBODIN'S MACKENZIE DISTRICT REPORT OF 1966

At first glance, and having read Ed's review, I experienced some shock and disappointment at the change in style and subject from the preface. Very dry stuff.... [W]hat the government needed to know, no doubt, but where are the people and their "rules of engagement" about living with each other—and about engaging with their natural environment? And isn't the style rather "cut-and-dried" (as we used to say, last century)? More like a census?

Reading further—and further—finally satisfied the two points in which I had most interest. The *first* was the inclusion in this formal report of a focus on the difficulty of defining a Metis group, or "culture," among the "ethnic populations" that anthropologists observe and describe. How did he choose the individuals counted under the "Metis" columns in his tables? His final chapter, "Metis Identity," sounds promising and should shed light at least vis-à-vis the Mackenzie, but the problem seems to run throughout.

The first chapter, "'Mixed' Populations," defines and provides a history of this type of population—worldwide first, and taking in several

varieties of racial mixtures. It then narrows in focus to North America
and reviews what has been published on the subject—most of it being concerned "understandably" with political and economic history, and lacking
"adequate scholarly treatment of the culture and society of the Metis in
themselves." The "understandably" gets us to a Canadian perspective,
pointing to "the formation of la nation metisse, the Northwest Insurrec-
tions of 1870 and 1885 and the political repercussions thereof" (7). As will
be seen, his dealing with my first point can be found most directly in his
first and last chapters. What he does about the lacking ethnographic treatment of the culture and society, in terms of the Mackenzie Metis (and
how he managed to be "among" them) must show up in the chapters in
between.

That is my second point: How much on-the-spot ethnography—or
what kind—is provided here? Scanning through all the dry numbers and
systematic lists and tables—which seem made to provide the extent and
type of government responsibility needed—leaves one still wondering.[5]
Ed Rogers listed twenty tables, named the nine chapters plus two appendices,[6] and had the nerve to add, "Extensive material is given in the chapters, so that one gets an extremely clear picture of how the Metis really
live" (Rogers 1967: 274). I thought, "From all those tables that simply
count how many of everything? I'd better start reading those chapters."
And so I did.

In the second chapter, "Regional Distinctions," Slobodin names and
describes the seven communities he chose to visit, for report data (his
fieldwork—although he generally terms this "conversations and interviews" or "visits and interviews"; Ed called it "his fieldnotes"). He notes
his omission of the city of Yellowknife, on the shores of Great Slave Lake,
as its greater size and complexity would require a longer presence than his
time allowed. A map of the Mackenzie District appears opposite his page 1.

One finds Great Slave Lake, close to the southern border of the district.
Dick chose Fort Resolution, on the southern side of the lake, instead of Yellowknife, to visit in 1963. This map can be compared with another one,
entitled "The Metis Landscape" from the 1980s (see below), to give a hint
about what is to come. The communities chosen by Slobodin were divided
between the southern portion of the district and the northern, as he already
knew these differed in important respects. He states elsewhere that most
of the field data for this report was collected during 1963 but that his
acquaintance with the area and its people had begun much earlier.[7]

Sure enough, table 1 (on page 26) shows the "ethnic composition" of
each of the studied communities—in four columns that give the numbers

of "Metis," "Indian," "Eskimo," and "White." (The author's own footnote
on page 6 states that the "Metis" in this district could include persons
with "African or American Negro, Japanese, Polynesian and Micronesian
non-indigenous ancestors.") His table 2 (on page 27) gives population figures for each community. There follows a description of each, with a generous supply of history, underlining and explaining the cultural and lifestyle
differences between north and southwhich appear related to their different histories.

Slobodin's ethnography comes largely through his comparison of the
"northern Metis" of the district and the southern Metis, the latter sometimes termed the "Metis proper" or the "Red River Metis." Two items of
comparison, as examples: the first, residence patterns, has Mackenzie's
northern people residing more stably, as a group, while the southern moved
frequently and consequently could travel more easily, having "relatives"
to stay with wherever they went. The second item: Red River Metis have
"autonomous Metis traditions" from an earlier period—the "Metis 'nation'
of the old Northwest" and the fur trade war—while the northern Metis
have "little autonomous Metis tradition," just from "the Hudson's Bay
Company period in the northern Mackenzie District" and "the aboriginal
society to which they are related." (This is a preview of the author's final
chapter, where his page 158 provides a "schematic summary" of ten "major
social and cultural distinctions" between these two populations in the
Mackenzie District—which then functions as his springboard for probing
some types of variations among Metis peoples in general, from an anthropological point of view.)

In chapter 3, "Sources of Data," the author is generous with his large
repertoire of available writings useful "for understanding the background
of Mackenzie Metis" but which expand to other regions of western Canada
and include works that he does not consider so useful; these are "all frankly
partisan and to be used with circumspection as sources of history or ethnography, but all, as labours of love or animus, filled with vivid detail."

His exceptions are Giraud (1945) and Howard (1952), as both "include
much information on Metis culture and society." It is clear he is familiar
with nearly all material in this category; his evaluations for their useful-
ness reflect ethnographic values as well as governmental.[8] It represents a
rather interesting bibliography of works available up to the 1960s. (His
own references at the end of the book are worth scanning also, if you have
the time.)

The second half of chapter 3 concentrates on the local sources used
for this study, with some detail, including "informants" and others, non-

Metis, from whom he received information and data. Finally, a section of acknowledgements, naming "those who have put me under obligation for kindness...."

The remaining chapters live up to their titles (see notes 5 and 6) and contain many tables accompanied by the fruit of "interviews" and "visits and discussions"—one might label some as "stories"[9]—that provide criteria on which the column choices were made and vital information of an ethnographic nature from local informants. Indeed, the reader does learn quite a lot about "how the Metis really live" (Rogers, 1967) in the Mackenzie District of the early 1960s, even from these chapters with tables created for the government.

Rogers's remark, however, probably included the chapter just preceding the last, which is entitled "External Relations" and contains no tables. It does, however, contain the answers to my questions on the social environment in which the district Metis carried on their lives and how they coped with it; about the changes in this environment—contrasting past and current periods and introducing the categories of the "externals" (non-Metis) they had to relate to, with incidents and conversations illustrating each.

There are also extended intellectual analyses of these topics, often headed with a term I would have had to look up in a dictionary (had the author not kindly defined it as used). An example can be found on page 140: "The Rationalization of Interpersonal Relations" is explained as "a working rationale" or agreed-upon structuring of particular relationships (my "rules of engagement," above?). An interesting finding: he proposes that Mackenzie Metis groups, while exhibiting internal rules, typically do not have a leader to deal with non-Metis as such—Fort Resolution being the one exception, for certain reasons.

The chapter begins, in fact, with his justification for the Metis as a proper subject for anthropological study—which I have cited in note 5. It also sets the stage for some of the topics that enrich the following final chapter, introducing the terms "tangential society" and providing a prelude to "agents and products of acculturation." It is interesting to note his way of "edging up" to a subject or an idea—like planting a seed, then returning to its flowering.

The final chapter, "Metis Identity," is richly replete with winding up and moving on. It becomes clear that Slobodin did manage both to separate and to combine the ethnographic and the government "census" type of information. (See note 5.)

He now proceeds to an added bonus, from his long acquaintance with the Mackenzie area and people, by relating changes that were taking place at the time of his writing, which seems to imply that much of what he had just reported would soon become a record of the past. Thus, first, summaries of the foregoing data, then an account of current changes, and then a look into the future—as that tail starts wagging again.

The first section, "Self Identification," sheds light on the difficulties in choosing particular persons for the "Metis" category of his tables; the second section explains the differences and reasons for separating his northern and southern groupings—these are then summarized grandly in the schematic chart on page 158, from which we find the edging up to "tangential" and the seed of his calculations on where anthropology's responsibilities lie in all this.

His look to the future thus includes a fresh examination of, and rumination on, the place of Metis studies in our discipline, targeting first its concept of "acculturation," which he feels presents difficulties if applied to the Mackenzie District Metis, where "the Metis are themselves both products and agents of acculturation" (page 159). This idea he explores here, "for Metis culture, insofar as it is distinctive, is itself a phenomenon of acculturation." One will see that he does not let go of these new thoughts, for they soon blossomed into his paper published later the same year (1964), after the end of the government contract. It is entitled "Subarctic Metis as Products and Agents of Culture Contact."

Postscript: Through the Decades

I became more interested in how Dick Slobodin's contribution to Metis studies fared in the remaining decades of the century, especially the effect of his parting shot in the final chapter, in which he defined "Metis Identity" (in terms of cultural or ethnic populations) as being "tangentially" related to an established culture (and likewise to anthropology?). Thus, like a limb of a tree, touching tangentially, at an angle—part of (more than just "rubbing elbows with") a cohesive culture?

Notes

1 The personal and professional traits reported by others who had known Dick longer and better than I are clearly evident in this "practical" report to the Canadian government, to meet their lack of information on mixed-blood residents of the far northwest corner of the country. The 1966 book here reviewed was published by the Canadian Research Centre for Anthropology, Saint-Paul University, Ottawa. The author's note on the title page states, "It is reproduced here as a contribution to our knowledge of the North." He adds: "The

opinions expressed, however, are those of the author and not necessarily those of the Department."

2 Sadly, one of the ways I did not know Dick Slobodin well was in my never having been blessed with any of his "stories." To make up for that, I am happy to pass along the words of a former student at McMaster University that I received in an email exchange when I told him of Dick's passing. Jim Daschuk replied as follows:

> I am sorry to hear about Dick Slobodin. He was my prof. in a circumpolar course when I was in first year at Mac, which was, yikes, 26 years ago. He would sit in a chair in front of a small class and tell us really good camping stories & I think smoked a pipe. I even got [a good mark] on the final exam for his class after I told him about seeing some miners from Timmins that I knew, growing marijuana when I was in Baffin.

Asked if he'd mind my using his story in my presentation honouring Dick, he replied: "I would be honoured if you used that story.... I was a kid fresh off the turnip truck from Timmins when I took his circumpolar class. I used to love it, he'd sit at the front, with his white goatee, and tell us excellent stories about the 'old days.'"

3 I speak both for myself and for my late husband and co-researcher, Edward S. Rogers, who, I now learned, had been a reviewer of this report (Rogers, 1967). However, I cannot speak for Ed as fully as I would like, since he had known Dick for some years before recruiting me to come from California for a two-year assignment for the Canadian government in subarctic Ontario in 1968. As it turned out, we worked together on that assignment until 1988, when Ed's life was ended by cancer.

4 The "joint work" of E.S. Rogers and M. Black-Rogers is known as the "Round Lake Study: 1958–1998," a long-term ethnographic-ethnohistorical record of a fly-in community in the subarctic Shield area of northwestern Ontario (now renamed Weagamow Lake). Research records, photographs, tape recordings, and database materials are being accessioned at the University of Alberta Archives, where a Finding Aide should soon be available.

5 I later found Slobodin's explanation regarding his ethnographic component in chapter 8 at page 135, as follows: "Ethnographies describing the present situation of northern peoples are likely to scant such time-honoured rubrics as 'Material Culture' and 'Ceremonial Life' in favour of 'Dependency' and 'Drinking Behaviour.' It is also true that the Metis have not constituted an independent society ... but have comprised, rather, a rural, or at any rate, a backwoods proletariat. Nevertheless, the most valid basis for an initial study of the Mackenzie District Metis lies within the tradition of social and cultural anthropology: consideration of them as humans who have worked out and are working out some means of living within the limitations of their ecology and their culture.... Some of their 'problems,' in terms of our social norms and requirements, should become apparent from such a study, while others may be scrutinized in special studies after a groundwork has been laid."

6 The list of chapter titles and appendix titles are from Ed Rogers's review: "The volume is divided into nine chapters: 'Mixed Populations,' 'Regional

Distinctions and Community Settings,' 'Sources of Data,' 'The Family," "Kinship,' 'Occupations,' 'Education,' 'External Relations,' and 'Metis Identity.'
In addition, there are two appendices and twenty tables" (1967: 274). The
appendices are titled "Ethnicity of Lovers and Spouses" and "Native Languages of District Metis."

7 Previous visits included not only the canoe trips of 1938–39 but also "field-
trips" of 1961–62 and earlier, although not for Metis research. Citing from his
chapter on sources: "Fieldnotes, memories, and—it is to be hoped—under-
standings accumulated during sojourns in the North between 1938 and 1962
provided a background which, it is felt, was indispensable to acquisition and
assimilation of material collected during 1963" (30). Slobodin's in-depth work
as anthropologist with the Kutchin (Gwich'in) Indians of this area constitutes
his chief ethnographic contribution, which I have heard described as "simply
outstanding." It is summarized in his chapter (No. 514) of the *Handbook of
North American Indians*, Vol. 6, *Subarctic* (1981). This volume also contains
his chapter dealing with "Subarctic Metis" (No. 361). In the latter he cites this
1966 report as the main source.

8 In the chapter on his sources, Slobodin prefers, among travellers and journal-
ists in the West, the American journalist Julian Ralph (1892), who "describes
the fur-trade Metis with sobriety and a good deal of sympathy" (as opposed
to most other writers, who were "contemptuous" of the "half-breed"). He
applauds Ralph's inclusion of numerous sketches by Frederic Remington and
uses a Remington sketch himself as frontispiece. My sister, an artist, has told
me that Remington has been described by art critic Robert Hughes (1997:
205) as a mere "illustrator" and not an artist. This may be the very reason he
appealed to Ralph, as well as to Slobodin and to me.

9 Dick's "legendary" habit of telling stories apparently did not affect his reputation as a scholar. I wonder if he perhaps learned this from the Indians. Here
is a story from my field experience:

> One of my bilingual informant-teachers in northern Minnesota was an eld-
> erly man who often responded to my (deliberately yes/no) questions with
> "I'll tell you a story about that." This would consume precious time for
> me—I was due back to university to finish my dissertation— but I was con-
> demned to listen to (and tape-record) all of his stories. Learning that this
> was "the way they do it" was a valuable part of the ethnographic data. And
> I harvested a fine crop of recorded stories. A bonus—although sometimes
> it took additional time to get it straight how the story answered the ques-
> tion—which produced another bonus: learning something about their
> cognitive connections: why the particular question had triggered that
> story. (This kind of fieldwork learning is what makes me currently suspi-
> cious of "virtual cultures" for ethnography students. I was one of the doc-
> toral students at Stanford in the 1960s who viewed our latest systematic
> field procedures, "ethnoscience," as a progressive step; but it didn't exclude
> the main ingredient: Being There.)

REFERENCES

Black-Rogers, Mary. 1991. "Review of *From the Land of Shadows: The Making of Grey Owl* by Donald B. Smith." *American Indian Culture and Research Journal* 15(3): 98–103.

———. 1998. "Picking Up the Threads: Metis History in the Mackenzie Basin." Metis Heritage Association of the Northwest Territories.

Dickason, Olive Patricia. 1984. "From 'One Nation' in the Northeast to 'New Nation' in the Northwest: A Look at the Emergence of the Métis." In Peterson and Brown, eds., *The New Peoples.*

Giraud, Marcel. 1945. "Le Metis Canadien: Son rôle dans l'histoire des provinces de l'ouest." *Travaux et Mémoires de l'Institut d'Ethnologie* 44.

Howard, Joseph Kinsey. 1952. *Strange Empire.* New York: Murrow.

Honigmann, John J. 1981. "Modern Subarctic Indians and Metis." In June Helm, ed., *Handbook of North American Indians.* Vol. 6: *The Subarctic,* 712–17. Washington, DC: Smithsonian Institution.

Hughes, Robert. 1997. *American Visions: The Epic History of Art in America.* New York: Knopf.

Peterson, Jacqueline, and Jennifer S.H. Brown, eds. 1984. *The New Peoples: Being and Becoming Métis.* Winnipeg: University of Manitoba Press.

Ralph, Julian. 1892. *On Canada's Frontier.* Illus. Frederic Remington. New York: Harper & Brothers.

Rogers, Edward S. 1967. "Review of *Metis of the Mackenzie District,* R. Slobodin, 1966." *Arctic* 20(4): 274.

Sawchuk, Joe. 1978. *The Métis of Manitoba: Reformulation of an Ethnic Identity.* Canadian Experience Series. Toronto: Peter Martin Associates.

Slobodin, Richard. 1960. "Some Social Functions of Kutchin Anxiety." *American Anthropologist* 62(1): 122–33.

———. 1964. "Subarctic Metis as Products and Agents of Culture Contact." *Arctic Anthropology* 2(2): 50–55.

———. 1966. *Metis of the Mackenzie District.* Ottawa: Canadian Research Centre for Anthropology.

———. 1981. "Subarctic Metis." In June Helm, ed., *Handbook of North American Indians,* Vol. 6: *The Subarctic,* 361–71. Washington, DC: Smithsonian Institution.

———. 1981. "Kutchin." In June Helm, ed., *Handbook of North American Indians,* Vol. 6: *The Subarctic,* 361–71, 514–32. Washington, DC: Smithsonian Institution.

Smith, Donald B. 1990. *From the Land of Shadows: The Making of Grey Owl.* Saskatoon, SK: Western Producer Prairie Books.

CHAPTER SEVEN

Richard Slobodin and the Creation of the *Amerindian Rebirth* Book

Antonia Mills

I remember Richard Slobodin particularly for his contribution to the tome *Amerindian Rebirth: Reincarnation Belief among North American Indians and Inuit* (Mills and Slobodin, 1994). I met with Dick on only two occasions: the session of the Canadian Anthropology Society/Société Canadienne d'Anthropologie (CASCA) on reincarnation among North American Indians that led to the book, and then when he came to Charlottesville, Virginia, for four or five days (as I recall) to work with me on the subsequent book.

I knew Dick first through his writings (Slobodin, 1960, 1962, 1969, 1970), some of which I can imagine I had read in preparation for starting fieldwork with the Beaver or Duneza of northeastern British Columbia in 1964. Writing this paper has been a fascinating integration of new knowledge I have gained about Dick, from the excellent obituaries written by Harvey Feit (2005a, 2005b) and David Damas (2005) to the array of knowledge available online, with my attempts to reconstruct by memory our face-to-face interaction on those two important and memorable occasions. The first of these was in 1990 and the second during our collaborative work session of a few days in (I think) 1993. This exercise in reconstructive memory has itself been compelling, not only because it has shown me how easy it is to project backwards and forwards slightly distorted or incorrect memories, but also because it has revealed how much of our experience of one another is based not on personal interaction solely but on reading texts written to a general public and on letters (or email, these days) or written text, which convey just as forcefully a sense of the person. Inevitably we amalgamate from these various sources to form a composite image of one another. I hope my rather specialized interaction with Dick will add to our collective memory of him.[1]

I have only recently come to learn how aspects of Dick's and my experience paralleled each other, a generation apart; that he was about twenty-three when in 1936 he went trekking across the north, which led to his serendipitous meeting and interaction with the Kutchin and changed the trajectory of his life toward anthropology. My meeting of the Dunneza in 1964, when I was twenty-two, did the same for me.[2] I was impressed by what Dick wrote regarding reincarnation experiences among the Kutchin, also known as the Gwich'in, which was a topic I learned about through the Dunneza, and a topic that my anthropological education had not prepared me to expect.[3] In subsequently working on my doctoral thesis, "The Beaver Indian Prophet Movement and Similar Movements among North American Indians" (1982), I sought to see how common the tenets of Beaver Indian philosophy were among other First Nations, reincarnation being one of them. I was impressed by Slobodin's fascinating depictions of Gwich'in past-life and come-back experiences (Slobodin, 1970, 1981).

I did not meet the author of these fine texts until 1990, when we both presented papers in the session called "Reincarnation among North American Indians" at the CASCA Conference in Calgary, Alberta. Were we the co-organizers of the session? In writing this paper I noted that my CV says I was the chair and co-organizer of it. But Dick does not claim to be co-organizer in his preface to *Amerindian Rebirth*. There he says, "It was Dr. Antonia Mills who introduced me to the fascinating enterprise of editing the present collection" (Mills and Slobodin, 1994: vii). In fact, my first interaction with Dick took place the previous year, when we or I (or was it someone else and I?) had put together a session for the American Anthropological Association on that same topic with many of the same presenters, including Jean-Guy Goulet, Edith Turner, Lee Guemple, Michael Harkin, and James Matlock, as I recall. But I did not get to meet Dick in 1989, because the session was not accepted.[4] Although I had not yet met Dick, I clearly recall his disappointment. He was disappointed not only that our important subject was spurned but also that the fees he had paid as part of the submission process were not to be refunded despite the rejection. Dick told or wrote me then that he was living on a pension. I now appreciate from the obituary of David Damas (2005) that Dick's pension was based on only seventeen years of employment, which was a result of Dick's having been on McCarthy's blacklist.[5] Not until our second meeting did

Source: *ARCTIC* 58, no. 4: 438.

Dick describe to me this personal history, the economic insecurity it engendered, and the empathy he felt for the disadvantaged clients with whom he worked as a social worker during the time he was *persona non grata* thanks to Joe McCarthy.

Thus, the session at the Calgary CASCA of 1990 on reincarnation among North American Indians was the reincarnation of the session intended for AAA in 1989 in Washington, DC, and it afforded my first personal meeting with Dick—and what a delightful meeting it was. Dick was both charming and very professional; he gave a polished paper and was delightful at the dinner that many of the presenters enjoyed that evening. I got to experience first-hand his charm at recounting poignant vignettes from his experiences with the Gwich'in and elsewhere.[6]

From that meeting on, it was clear to me that I wanted Dick to co-edit the subsequent book *Amerindian Rebirth: Reincarnation Belief among North American Indians and Inuit,* which grew out of the Calgary CASCA conference. I looked forward to his input and enthusiasm and had a sense that his solid reputation would enhance the book and make it more accessible to the public were the same book to be edited only by me, Dick's junior and someone whose anthropological career had been interrupted for

almost as many years as Dick's, although because of different circumstances.[7] To my pleasure, Dick enthusiastically agreed to be co-editor.
Much of our initial communication on the project was by phone or through
letters, but once the book was accepted for publication by the University
of Toronto Press we needed to sit down together to make some important
collaborative decisions on its form and intent and structure. To this end,
Dick applied for and received a grant from the Arts Research Board at
McMaster University for a travel subvention to come to Charlottesville for
four or five days, as I recall.

Dick's Charlottesville visit was my second and much more extensive
meeting with him. Dick stayed in the "lab" associated with the Division
of Personality Studies at the University of Virginia, which was part of the
Department of Behavioral Medicine and Psychiatry.[8] Ian Stevenson, an
M.D. and psychiatrist famous for his studies of "cases of the reincarnation
type" not only among North American Indians but also among the Igbo
of Nigeria, the Alevi of Turkey, the Druse of Lebanon, and elsewhere
(Stevenson 1974, 1975a, 1975, 1977, 1980, 1983, 1987, 1997a, 1997b,
2000), was director of the Division of Personality Studies.[9] Ian and Dick
met first in Dr. Stevenson's office during Dick's visit. They were a perfectly
matched pair, both erudite scholars with an element of Old World formality, coupled with a sharp intellect and dry sense of humour, and they
had a commonality of interests, including W.H.R. Rivers. There was an
instant rapport and respect between the two. As I recall, they met again
at the division's weekly lunch and at a gracious dinner at Dr. Stevenson's
antebellum home. It was during these occasions, and also while Dick and
I worked together that week, that Dick told me many vignettes of his life.
Finances were still an issue, so he graciously accepted eating supper at my
UVA faculty housing home with my youngest son, to whom he played a
kindly grandparental role. How I wish I had the mental capacity to play
back to myself, and to you, an accurate tape recording of all he said!
Although I don't, I will try.

I want to recount first some of the stories Dick told that stand out in
my memory of his Charlottesville visit that added appreciably to my knowledge of this man I knew largely from reading his published works. Some
of the stories Dick told were accounts of Gwich'in rebirth cases, particularly of Black Tom, the African American slave who made his way to the
Arctic, bearing on his back the scars of the whippings he had received, and
who subsequently was reborn as a Gwich'in baby girl, who was a matron
when Dick met her. Some of my memories are of his description of his
heritage, which as I recall contained some Russian Jewish background and

a complex trajectory of his family to the "New World" (another quote-unquote, as Dick knew so well); still others describe his experiences in New York as both a young and mature adult, including eating bagels in his favourite delicatessen shops. One of my most poignant memories was Dick's depiction of the kindness of Margaret Mead in encouraging his return to New York and his work toward a Ph.D. He told about her giving him office space in which to work—was it at Columbia or at the American Museum of Natural History? I have forgotten, but my mind still holds the images Dick conveyed of a dark, book-lined, wood-panelled office that contained Margaret Mead and Franz Boas and many other materials, and Mead moving a typewriter so Dick could have a desk area to call his own. How I wish I could recall all he told about Boas encounters, his own and those of others! The prime story he related was how Boas invited Dick and a number of scholars, including Levi-Strauss, to lunch and then proceeded to expire while sitting upright at the table. Through our Charlottesville time together Dick also interwove a few stories of his kids and particularly of Eleanor, his wife, who survives him, and depictions of their heritage home next to one previously inhabited by Henry Schoolcraft, the geographer and ethnologist who expired in 1864. Eleanor and Dick apparently had extensive conversations there about the narratives involved in the *Amerindian Rebirth* book. From that Charlottesville visit, I owe to Eleanor the first part of the title of my future book, *"That's My Chair": Rebirth Narratives of the Gitxsan and Witsuwit'en*.[10]

The work with Dick on issues regarding the *Amerindian Rebirth* book was mutually satisfying. We needed to make decisions on a variety of concerns, such as which chapters—from the various scholars we had solicited to write in light of the University of Toronto Press readers' reviews—to include and exclude; our mutual translation of the chapter by Bernard Saladin-d'Anglure from French to English; and, particularly, the tone the book was to take on the topic of rebirth. Regarding chapters, we argued for the inclusion of one chapter the UTP readers had argued against, and accepted exclusion of two others. Ironically, the chapter by Alexander von Gernet stayed in.[11]

During Dick's Charlottesville visit, the most significant aspect that we hashed out was how to handle the manuscript reviewers' suggestion to divide the book into two parts, one that described First Nations rebirth experiences as belief, without looking at the whether it represents evidence, and one that took the indigenous perspective and considered whether cases represented evidence that supports the concept. In that context, I learned how much Dick cared about the topic and how much he wanted to express the Gwich'in thoughts on the subject. His willingness to take their experience seriously rather then simply metaphorically shows a level of openness and appreciation that it is important to honour.[12] We concluded that the initial chapters from the 1990 CASCA session, and the addition of a foreword by Gananath Obeyesekere comparing Buddhist, Hindu, and Jain eschatologies to Trobriand and North American; a reprint of the late Paul Radin's work on the reincarnations of Thunder Cloud, a Winnebago Indian; additional chapters by a diversity of anthropologists such as Mark Nuttall and von Gernet; and a chapter by psychiatrist Ian Stevenson on the Haida, did not lend themselves to such a division. As we worked towards this agreement, the integrity that he manifested through the difficult time of being McCarthy-banned, about which I had just learned, seemed to me to be shining through again. In his final edition of the final chapter for *Amerindian Rebirth*, chapter 16, "The Study of Reincarnation in Indigenous American Culture," Dick concluded by supporting the scientific study of cases, à la Stevenson, despite its suspect nature in Western academe, while noting that he had not thought Gwich'in cases, in terms of evidence when he had undertaken a systematic study, were odd or different. He said,

> To entertain the possibility of the reality of reincarnation is to look towards the farther shore of an epistemological Rubicon. Searchers for this reality wish, it would seem, to venture into
>
> The undiscovered country from whose bourne
>
> No travellers returns....
>
> ... To most scientists or scholarly researchers this may well seem on a par with those attempts at logical proof of God's existence which since Kant have been regarded as out of place in our professional endeavours. (Slobodin, 1994: 295)

But he goes on to say,

> I see no necessity for the interdiction of rationally organized efforts at examining claims for the survival of some aspect of the personality subsequent to the bearer's physical death. Indeed to refrain from examining these claims as real evidence, to regard them as folklore in situations where the beliefs are strongly held and tightly organized, is open to two kinds of objection. First, such abstention reflects a superior, de haut en bas attitude toward the convictions of one's informants. Second, it is a turning away, on dogmatic grounds, from an inviting trail of investigation into important and interesting possibilities.... As to the second objection, I fail to see why such investigation is not to be regarded as rational research, especially if it is conducted with the scrupulous care shown by F.W.H. Myers

in the late nineteenth century and by Ian Stevenson in recent decades. (Slobodin, 1994: 295–96)

Slobodin notes, "Those who have kept an open mind on the question of evidence for reincarnation have not abandoned functionalist, structuralist, or others types of explanation." Further: "Guemple, Radin, Saladin d'Anglure, von Gernet, Mauze, Harkin, Nuttall, and I have presented a variety of perspectives which do not include the investigation of the actuality or reincarnation" (Slobodin, 1994: 296–97). He concludes:

> We urge readers of any and all dispositions to read these chapters with an open mind and to judge for themselves whether the approach derived from Stevenson's researches is antithetical to or detracts from the other ways of looking at studying belief in reincarnation among North American Native peoples. For myself, I have formed the opinion that we would do well to study reincarnation with great care, both for the knowledge and, in so far as we are capable of it, for enlightenment. (Slobodin, 1994: 297)

Dick's concluding chapter could have been silent on this issue.[13] But Dick knew that reincarnation formed an integral part of Gwich'in identity, and he was open to the concept that reincarnation plays an integral part in human nature, topics highlighted in this CASCA conference, despite noting that he had not thought about the Gwich'in case in terms of evidence while he was working with them. The result was the book that Harvey Feit described in his online obituary: "This is a widely cited work in anthropology and religious studies that explores its subject with the finesse required to respect indigenous peoples and to avoid comfortable but reductionist explanations" (Feit, 2005b).

The University of Toronto Press's statement about the book notes the stance taken, describing it thusly:

> Until now, few people have been aware of the prevalence of belief in some form of rebirth or reincarnation among North American native peoples. This collection of essays by anthropologists and one psychiatrist examines this concept among native American societies, from near the time of contact until the present day.
>
> *Amerindian Rebirth* opens with a foreword by Gananath Obeyesekere that contrasts North American and Hindu/Buddhist/Jain beliefs. The introduction gives an overview, and the first chapter summarizes the context, distribution, and variety of recorded belief. All the papers chronicle some aspect of rebirth belief in a number of different cultures. Essays cover such topics as seventeenth-century Huron eschatology, Winnebago ideology, varying forms of Inuit belief, and concepts of rebirth found among subarctic natives and Northwest Coast peoples.

The closing chapters address the genesis and anthropological study of Amerindian reincarnation. In addition, the possibility of evidence for the actuality of rebirth is addressed. *Amerindian Rebirth* will further our understanding of concepts of self-identity, kinship, religion, cosmology, resiliency, and change among native North American peoples. (http://www.utppublishing.com)

I did not see Dick again after his Charlottesville trip, but we stayed in close touch.[14] He was pleased to see the reviews of *Amerindian Rebirth*.[15] If, in the thick of grading at the end of term, I did not get my Christmas card sent to Dick and Eleanor, I heard from Dick! He told me, in one of his Christmas cards, about the publication of the second edition of his 1978 book on W.H.R. Rivers, commenting that Pat Barker's fictionalized trilogy on Rivers, *Regeneration* (1993a), *The Eye in the Door* (1993b), and *The Ghost Road* (1995), had increased public interest in Rivers and led to the second edition.[16] Dick's appreciation of Rivers was something he had in common with Ian Stevenson and was part of their instant rapport. They shared an interest not only in Rivers but in his contemporaries and colleagues William James and Frederick Myers.

I think the last thing I received from Dick was a copy of his article on Rivers and those who have depicted him, called "Who Would True Valor See" (Slobodin, 1998). It reminds me of why Dick took such an interest in describing Rivers' work; Rivers, like Dick, was interested in psychology and ethnology, in kinship and social organization, and in recovery from traumatic experience. In Dick's 1998 article, he notes that neither his nor Langham's depiction of Rivers captures the whole man. "History and biography are crafted writings in which events and characters are presented in retrospect and in relation to some organizing idea," he says. "This perspective is strikingly different from the events or the life as perceived by the protagonists while they are unfolding" (Slobodin, 1998: 305). How telling that I have found the same thing in trying to construct my memories of my experience of Dick.

In 1999 I went to Whitehorse to give a paper at the Canadian Archaeology Society conference and was delighted to meet a number of Gwich'in elders there. Charlie Peter Charlie was one of these elders. They all had fond memories of Dick, asked after his health, and of course asked if he would be coming to the conference. They were sorely disappointed that he was not. I told them about the *Amerindian Rebirth* book, and they smiled and said the deceased elders were still coming back. Dick Preston's presentation of Dene appreciations adds to the enigma of the way Dick is recognized as a relative.

It is a pleasure to learn from one anothers' depictions and experiences of Dick. Limited as my experience with him was, it was important, if shorter than I would have liked. Frankly, I was shocked when I came across an obituary for Richard Slobodin in the *Anthropology Newsletter* in the fall of 2005, for I had no idea that he had expired months before, on January 22, 2005. I was surprised that I had not heard that this had happened. I was consoled by the fact that he had indeed reached a venerable age, just short of ninety. I feel for Eleanor. Dick and I both knew that even in cultures that have complete faith in rebirth, mourning for the deceased is not lessened. But it does put "concepts of self-identity, kinship, religion, cosmology, resiliency, and change," to quote from Mills and Slobodin (1994), in the context of rebirth eschatologies.

NOTES

1 Dick was familiar with the vagaries of memory, noting, "How close a resemblance, one may wonder, did the Pacific campaign he later recollected in tranquility, or that of any of us there recollected, bear to the events we experienced as they occurred?"

2 Dick's serendipitous trip with a friend following his M.A., as you know from other papers on Dick, led to his return and enrolment in a doctoral program in anthropology at Columbia University in 1922. I began my undergraduate studies in anthropology forty years later as a result of a different serendipitous trip to Trinidad and South America as the nanny for the daughter of Robert Lowell and Elizabeth Hardwick. At the mouth of the Amazon River, where we were the guests of a Brazilian poet and his (quote-unquote) "Indian princess wife," I thought, "What am I doing studying French history and literature? I want to learn about all the cultures of the world!" At that time and place (Recife, Brazil), I had a tremendous sense of the power of the indigenous cultures steaming up and down the Amazon, and went back and was accepted into anthropology as my major before I'd taken a single course.

In beginning anthropology classes that fall as a junior at Harvard/Radcliffe, I met Robin Ridington, who was just beginning a Ph.D. in anthropology as a result of having met the Beaver Indians, or Dunneza, when he went to the Peace River of northern British Columbia to help fellow and former Swarthmore students who had learned that they could homestead Crown land and make it their own by "improving" it. While building a cabin—the thing that would constitute the improvement—they and Robin learned that what they thought was Crown land was in fact right in the middle of Beaver Indian traditional territory. Like Slobodin, Robin began a career in anthropology based on this experience with northern Dene. My marriage to Robin at the beginning of my senior year meant that I did my so-called fieldwork with the Dunneza with Robin rather than going to Chiapas as Dr. Evan Vogt had suggested. All these pieces of serendipitous contact with indigenous peoples thus led first

Slobodin, then Robin Ridington, and then me to careers in anthropology and
to coming to know the northern Athapaskans.

3   I was equally surprised to learn, when I arrived with my former husband (and
first ex) Robin Ridington in 1964, that the Dunneza had a living prophet.
While prophet movements and belief in reincarnation have not gone undoc-
umented or unexplored in ethnological writings, what literature I had read
had not prepared me to expect either of these two phenomena to exist among
the contemporary Dunneza.

4   It is interesting to note that of the succession of presentations at conferences
that my CV reveals I had given prior to the 1990 Calgary conference, five of
seven were on the topic of Amerindian reincarnation. These papers led to a
number of publications, namely, Mills 1994b, 1988a, 1988b, 1986. I continue
to work on First Nations land claims (Mills, 1994a, 2005b) and on rebirth
(Mills, 2001, 2005a; Mills, Matchatis, and Hill 2005). In the eyes of the First
Nations peoples, the two topics are integrally related.

5   I think that at the time he was not a member of AAA—I do not recall if he had
joined (or rejoined) in the expectation of attending the conference; in any
case, he was looking forward to coming. The aborted AAA session of 1989 and
the unrefunded money issue was my first personal experience with Dick,
though only through letters and phone calls, as he did not use email and had
to go to McMaster to do any work on a computer, as I recall. He preferred
the typewriter. I now appreciate that his pain at our rejection was perhaps not
only financial but a throwback to the setbacks he had experienced from uni-
versities' inability to employ him during the McCarthy era, when he was finan-
cially responsible for a growing family.

6   As I recall, the 1990 Calgary CASCA was also my first meeting with Jean-
Guy Goulet, who was equally charming at the dinner afterwards. Another
person who made it a point to attend the Calgary session was the late Beatrice Medicine, which led to a subsequent session at the AAA in Washington
with Jean-Guy Goulet, Beatrice Medicine, and an impressive number of
Native Americans addressing aspects of two-spirit culture, a topic I do not
recall discussing with Dick, although cross-gendered rebirth was part of the
"Black Tom" case.

7   Serendipitous encounters that led to anthropological studies and careers were
not the only life experience Dick and I had in common. A second commonality was the interruption of those anthropological careers. I had voluntarily
interrupted my anthropological career when my Ph.D. thesis supervisor,
Dr. John W.M. Whiting, informed me that the "publishable paper" I had sent
to him "was very beautiful and should be published but was not the distorted
monster a thesis was supposed to be." You have to understand that my first son
was born in 1967, the morning after my Ph.D. oral exams, and all I had left
to do was the "publishable paper," the statistics requirement, and the thesis.
In 1969, when John Whiting told me that my "publishable paper was not the
distorted monster a thesis is supposed to be," I was expecting baby No. 2 and
a distorted monster was the last thing I wanted to produce. Therefore, I silently
withdraw from the Ph.D. program, content to be doing work with the Dunneza with Robin. (The 1969 publishable paper, "Beaver Indian Supernatural

Power: The Cosmology of Consciousness," subsequently appeared, with additions by Robin Ridington, in 1970 as "The Inner Eye of Totemism and Shamanism" and was reprinted in 1975 in Dennis and Barbara Tedlock's *Teachings from the American Earth*.) I finally completed the thesis—another marriage and two more children later. I was surprised to learn from a calculation based on facts in Feit's obituary (2005b) that it had taken Dick nineteen years from the start to the finish of his doctorate (1940–59), because of the variety of interruptions and challenges. I calculated that mine took a mere eighteen (1964–82). During our 1993 Charlottesville visit, we compared notes on challenges and child-rearing responsibilities; obviously, Dick's challenge—that of being blacklisted by Joe McCarthy—exceeded my challenges as a sometimes single mother.

8   Like Rivers' "laboratory for experimental psychology at Cambridge" (Slobodin 1998: 300), fellow psychiatrist Stevenson had a laboratory for conducting experimental psychology behind the Division of Personality Studies at the University of Virginia. During the time I was there, it served only as accommodation for visiting scholars. Dick was only one of its distinguished guests.

9   Dr. Stevenson was responsible for creating the position of research assistant professor that I held at UVA for six years, with a cross-appointment as instructor in the anthropology department.

10 Eleanor suggested "That's My Chair" as the title of a chapter or section of the book *Amerindian Rebirth*, as I recall. However, it works particularly well for the book I worked on subsequently. It contains the story of the preschool Gitxsan girl who came into her grandmother's house and kicked her uncle out of a chair, saying, "That's *my* chair." In fact the chair had belonged to her maternal great-grandmother, the elder whom the young girl is said to re-embody. That account was first published in Mills (1988), and either Eleanor read it or Dick told her about it. *"That's My Chair"* is forthcoming.

11 I have never met von Gernet, and I do not think Dick had either. Fortunately Tom Flanagan has never written anything on reincarnation, so we did not include two chapters by anthropologists who testify against First Nations in land claims and treaty cases and who have had no personal contact with First Nations.

12 Dick was willing to express himself in this arena, although he was well aware of the intellectual positions that are used to reduce rebirth experience from the place it held, or holds, in the Gwich'in world. He enjoyed the task of editing his previously published material into chapter 9, "Kutchin Concepts of Reincarnation," which contains afterthoughts on his article of 1970. He also took pleasure in constructing the final and sixteenth chapter.

13 Dick said that Rivers, "in his desire to urge social/cultural anthropology toward the status of science, was rather too easily beguiled by likely or plausible causal relationships" (Slobodin, 1998: 305). Stevenson's work is considered suspect by some because it seeks to use the scientific method to assess explanations that do not fit into the Western materialist paradigm. Dick appreciated that reincarnation was a reality to the Gwich'in. Dick had been persecuted for socialist interests by McCarthy, and was not about to compromise his sense of what was acceptable and appropriate to investigate on the basis of others' concepts of acceptability.

14 I hoped to see him at the 1991 CASCA meetings at the University of Western Ontario, London, Ontario, where I gave a paper called "Cultural Contrast: The British Columbia Court's Evaluation of the Gitksan and Wetsuwet'en and Their Own Sense of Self and Self-Worth as Revealed in Cases of Reported Reincarnation." We had talked about my coming to see his heritage home in Hamilton, but it didn't happen. I sent him the paper when it was published (Mills, 1995). He always graciously acknowledged the articles I sent him.

15 The reviews of *Amerindian Rebirth* we discussed included those by James Frideres in *Canadian Journal of Native Studies* 15(1) (1996): 180–83; G. Oosten (University of Leiden) in *Inuit Studies* (1996): 123–26; Christopher Vecsey in *American Indian Culture and Research Journal* 19(2) (1995): 171–73; Jean Manore in *Social Science and Humanities Aboriginal Research Exchange* 3(2) (1996): 12–136; Ronald Niezen (Harvard University) in *American Ethnologist* 22(4) (1995): 1058; Ake Hultkrantz (University of Stockholm, Sweden) in *Ethnos* 60 (1995): 1–2, 140–43; Wayne A. Holst (Arctic Institute of North America) in *Culture* 14(2) (1994): 137–38; and R.G. Williamson in *Anthropologica* 36 (1994): 231–32.

16 The second edition of Dick's book on Myers currently (i.e., early May 2006) appears with two different covers on Amazon.com, one of them with a diagonal red band added to it that says, "As in Regeneration." It rated at four stars, while Pat Barker's novels are given four and a half stars. *Amerindian Rebirth* had five stars when I viewed it on May 7, 2006; the preceding day, Barker's trilogy and Slobodin's Rivers book had the same number of stars, but *Amerindian Rebirth* had none shown, and that delivery would take four to six weeks. It was a relief to see that had changed to what I had recalled from former Amazon.com excursions.

REFERENCES

Barker, Pat. 1993a. *The Eye in the Door*. New York: Penguin.
———. 1993b. *Regeneration*. New York: Plume/Penguin.
———. 1995. *The Ghost Road*. New York: Plume/Penguin.
Damas, David. 2005. "Obituary of Richard Slobodin." *Arctic* 5(4): 438–39. Retrieved May 6, 2006, from http://pubs.aina.ucalgary.ca/arctic/Arctic 58-4-438.pdf.
Feit, Harvey. 2005a. "Obituary of Richard Slobodin." *Anthropology Newsletter* 36(6): 52.
———. 2005b. "Obiturary of Dr. Richard Slobodin." Retrieved May 6, 2006, from http://www.mcmaster.ca/mufa/newsfeb-marcho5.html#slobodin.
Frideres, James. 1996. "Review of *Amerindian Rebirth*." *Canadian Journal of Native Studies* 15(1): 18083.
Holst, Wayne A. 1994. "Review of *Amerindian Rebirth*." *Culture* 14(2): 137–38.
Hultkrantz, Ake. 1995. "Review of *Amerindian Rebirth*." *Ethnos* 60(1–2): 140–43.
Manore, Jean. 1996. "Review of *Amerindian Rebirth*." *Social Science & Humanities Aboriginal Research Exchange* (SSHARE/ERASSH) 3(2): 12–13.

Mills, Antonia. 2005a. "Gitksan and Witsuwit'en Experience of the Boundaries of the Self: Body-Bounded or Spirit Bound?" *Journal of Religious Studies and Theology* 24(2): 81–116.

———, ed. 2005b. *"Hang on to These Words": Johnny David's* Delgamuukw *Testimony*. Toronto: University of Toronto Press.

———. 2001. "Sacred Land and Coming Back: How Gitxsan and Witsuwit'en Reincarnation Stretches Western Boundaries." *Canadian Journal of Native Studies* 21(1): 309–31.

———. 1994a. *Eagle Down Is Our Law: Witsuwit'en Laws, Feasts and Land Claims*. Vancouver: University of British Columbia Press.

———. 1994b. "Making a Scientific Investigation of Ethnographic Cases Suggestive of Reincarnation." In David Young and Jean-Guy Goulet, eds., *Being Changed: The Anthropological Experience*, 237–69. Peterborough, ON: Broadview Press.

———. 1995. "Cultural Contrast: The British Columbia Court's Evaluation of the Gitksan Witsuwit'en and Their Own Sense of Self and Self-Worth as Revealed in Cases of Reported Reincarnation." *BC Studies* (104): 149–72.

———. 1988a. "A Preliminary Investigation of Reincarnation among the Beaver and Gitksan Indians." *Anthropologica* 30(1): 23–59.

———. 1988b. "A Comparison of Witsuwit'en Cases of the Reincarnation Type with Gitksan and Beaver." *Journal of Anthropological Research* 44(4): 385–415.

———. 1986. "The Meaningful Universe: Intersecting Forces in Beaver Indian Cosmology and Causality." *Culture* 6(2): 81–91. Reprinted in David Miller, Carl Beal, James Dempsey, and R. Wesley Heber, eds., *The First Ones: Readings in Indian/Native Studies*, 226–33. Saskatoon: Saskatchewan Indian Federated College Press, 1992.

———. 1982. "The Beaver Indian Prophet Dance and Related Movements among North American Indians." Unpublished Ph.D. dissertation, Harvard University.

———. 1969. "Beaver Indian Supernatural Power: The Cosmology of Consciousness." Harvard unpublished "publishable paper."

Mills, Antonia, and Richard Slobodin, eds. 1994. *Amerindian Rebirth: Reincarnation Belief among North American Indians and Inuit*. Toronto: University of Toronto Press.

Mills, Antonia, Connie Matchatis, and Georgina Hill. 2005. "Ake Hultkrantz's Contributions to the Understanding of Souls, Their Return and Their Place in Shamanism Confirmed by Contemporary Cases." Special Issue in Honour of Ake Hultkrantz, *Shaman* 13(1–2): 95–114.

Niezen, Ronald 1995. "Review of *Amerindian Rebirth*." *American Ethnologist* 22(4): 1058.

Oosten, G. 1996. "Review of *Amerindian Rebirth*." *Inuit Studies* 19(20): 123–26.

Ridington, Robin, and Tonia Ridington (Mills). 1970. "The Inner Eye of Totemism and Shamanism." *History of Religions* 10(1): 49–61. Reprinted in D. and B. Tedlock, eds., *Teachings from the American Earth*. New York/Toronto: Liveright/George McLeod, 1975.

Slobodin, Richard. 1960. "Some Social Functions of Kutchin Anxiety." *American Anthropologist* 62(1): 122–33.

———. 1962. *Band Organization of the Peel River Kutchin.* National Museum of Canada Bulletin No. 179. Ottawa: Northern Affairs and National Resources

———. 1970. "Kutchin Concepts of Reincarnation." *Western Canadian Journal of Anthropology* 2(1): 67–79.

———. 1978. *W.H.R. Rivers.* New York: Columbia University Press.

———. 1989. "Follow the Drinking Gourd." *Northern Review* 3/4: 42–53.

———. 1994a. "Kutchin Concepts of Reincarnation." In Antonia Mills and Richard Slobodin, eds., *Amerindian Rebirth: Concepts of Reincarnation among North American Indians and Inuit,* 136–55. Toronto: University of Toronto Press.

———. 1994b. "Reincarnation among Indigenous American Cultures." In Antonia Mills and Richard Slobodin, eds., *Amerindian Rebirth: Concepts of Reincarnation among North American Indians and Inuit,* 284–97. Toronto: University of Toronto Press.

———. 1996. *W.H.R. Rivers: Pioneer Anthropologist, Psychiatrist of the Ghost Road.* New York: Allan Sutton Publishing.

———. 1998. "Who Would True Valor See." *History & Anthropology* 10(4): 299–317.

Stevenson, Ian. 1974. *Twenty Cases Suggestive of Reincarnation.* 2nd rev. ed. Charlottesville: University Press of Virginia.

———. 1975. *Cases of the Reincarnation Type.* Vol. 1: *Ten Cases in India.* Charlottesville: University Press of Virginia.

———. 1977. "The Southeast Asian Interpretation of Gender Dysphoria: An Illustrative Case Report." *Journal of Nervous and Mental Disease* 165: 201–208.

———. 1983. "American Children Who Claim to Remember Previous Lives." *Journal of Nervous and Mental Disease* 171: 742–48.

———. 1987. *Children Who Remember Previous Lives: A Question of Reincarnation.* Charlottesville: University Press of Virginia.

———. 1997a. *Reincarnation and Biology: A Contribution to the Etiology of Birthmarks and Birth Defects.* Vol. 1: *Birthmarks.* Westport, CT: Praeger.

———. 1997b. *Reincarnation and Biology: A Contribution to the Etiology of Birthmarks and Birth Defects.* Vol. 2: *Birth Defects and Other Anomalies.* Westport, CT: Praeger.

———. 2000. "Unusual Play in Young Children who Claim to Remember Previous Lives." *Journal of Scientific Exploration* 14: 557–70.

Vecsey, Christopher 1995. "Review of *Amerindian Rebirth.*" *American Indian Culture and Research Journal* 19(2): 171–73.

Williamson, R.G. 1994. "Review of *Amerindian Rebirth.*" *Anthropologica* 36: 231–32.

CHAPTER EIGHT

Richard Slobodin as Scholar of Societies

David J. Damas

Those of us who knew Dick think of him more as a humanist than a social scientist in the strictest sense of the latter term. We think of him more as a student of culture than of society. Yet, especially in his earlier writings, he made significant contributions to our understanding of Kutchin[1] social organization. His major work in this regard was *Band Organization of the Peel River Kutchin* (Slobodin, 1962: 45). This monograph did not immediately deal with matters of band organization. I think Dick was concerned with an ethnographic responsibility to record and report as much of people's lives as was possible, based on one's study of a given society and culture. It is also at least implicit that Dick thought the material provided in his long preamble to the subject in some way would relate to his main topic.

In his introduction we learn of Dick's historical orientation. Later, we will accept this perspective as intrinsically appropriate to the study of the Kutchin. Subsequent chapters deal with the physical setting and what a traveller will experience in the country and what her or his first impressions of its people will be (Slobodin, 1962: 7–15).

What follows are chapters on local history divided into phases, described by Dick as the proto-contact period, the Klondike gold rush period, and the muskrat period. Chapter 8 covers the main topic, Kutchin social organization (Slobodin, 1962: 42–46). The chapter begins with a brief description of the kinship system. There is a Hawaiian cousin system, equating all cousins with siblings, and an unusual combination of these cousins with a bifurcate collateral aunt–uncle system. Age differences are recognized on both Ego's and first ascending generations. Great attention is paid to wealth. "As maintenance of high status requires the support of kin this tendency I generally reciprocated," Dick writes. "This means that, in effect, high-ranking 'wealthy' men may have many kin, while poverty and lack of kin are nearly synonymous" (1962: 42).

The topic of behaviour among kin is treated in this chapter, especially with reference to respect and joking. Dick reports the presence of both initial matrilocality and matrilineal sibs. The origin of these sibs has been a matter of some debate. Steward (1955: 147) posited diffusion from the northwest coast. The ethnologists of the region differed in their view. McKennan (1969: 145) thought that matrilineality "was a very old practice." McClellan (1969: 115) agreed with this idea for the interior of Alaska but argued that sibs among the southern Tutchoni were diffused from the Tlingit. Slobodin posited that the matrilineal sibs among the Peel River Kutchin were a recent acquisition from the west. However old they might have been by the time of Dick's visits to the region, matrilineal sibs—which had in his view functioned mainly in the contacts with peoples to the west and south—were obsolescent. These latter views appear to have been supported by the statement of a Peel River woman interviewed by Dick in 1961: "As soon as these people (Southern Tutchone) meet, they ask are you a Wolf or a Crow? I say I am not a wolf or a crow, I'm a person" (Slobodin, 1962: 45).

The meat of Slobodin's depiction of the Peel River social organization comes with his presentation of types of groupings (Slobodin, 1962: 42–53, 54–57, 58–65, 66–72, 73–74). The smaller units were the local group and the trapping party. Both were composed of between four and eight nuclear families. That was about the only shared feature. The local group, as the name implies, was bound to a definite locality, while the trapping party moved from place to place, according to the exigencies of hunting and trapping. Duration of the local group was from one to two generations, while two months' duration was typical for a trapping party. The local group was essentially a bilocal extended family, and leadership was ascribed to the senior male (or at times to the senior female). Kinship connections within the trapping party, particularly in the one of which Dick was a member, were present as well but were highly irregular and often quite remote. Leadership was based on knowledge of the country to be travelled in, reputation for being a good traveller, and such personal qualities as "shrewdness and wiliness" balanced with "generosity and concern for the common weal" (Slobodin, 1962: 66).

In the band organization volume, Dick's description of the structure of the party was compact, with the author devoting as much space to characterization of the personnel as to the actual itinerary and activities of the party. We are given personality profiles of several of the members and of their interactions. To me, it is apparent that this face-to-face contact he enjoyed with the members of the party was more congenial to Dick's humanistic perspective than was his treatment of larger units. This is borne out in a later paper (Slobodin, 1969), "Leadership and Participation in a Kutchin Trapping Party." There he deals in greater detail with the structure and activities of the party of which he had been a member and much less with other types of groupings. Of course, it is possible to employ this person-by-person approach in small-scale situations, which in this case comprised only twenty-four persons. In the later publication, Dick retained his personal approach but developed matters touched upon earlier and introduced new aspects of the party's character and activities. One discussion that was expanded upon concerned the adoption of behaviour appropriate to people holding closer sorts of kinship roles than those that actually existed. This practice was apparently due to the narrow range of prescribed behavioural directives in Kutchin society. Thus, during the period of membership in the party, one could address and relate to such roles as brother, father, grandmother, brother-in-law, and sister-in-law, whereas the actual relationship might be more remote. In the later publication, he adds, "actually it [the trapping party] resembles the Kutchin local group, which is an extended family, more closely in function than in structure" (Slobodin, 1969a: 74). This is especially remarkable considering the contrast between the two types of units noted above.

In this paper, Dick provides a diagram that depicts those members of the trapping party who belonged to a unit, which is described as being a "quasi-kinship group" and which traced membership back to a prominent nineteenth-century chief. This designation eases somewhat the problem involved in looseness of kinship ties within the party, for fourteen of the seventeen adults belong to that descent group (Slobodin, 1969a: 72).

Moving to large groups, Dick cites the following: (1) the meat camp based on caribou hunting during the winter, (2) the fish camp associated with fishing during the summer, (3) the trading party, where people other that the Peel River Kutchin were encountered for trade, and (4) the band and its assembly. These groups vary in size from ten to fifty families, except for the band assembly, for which Dick indicated fifty to seventy families. In these larger groups, leadership was based mainly on wealth, though it is noted that the personal qualities cited for leadership in the small groups were also important. A diagram of a large camp from "premodern" times (Slobodin, 1962: 62) shows that both wealth and sib membership were involved in the placement of households. In another diagram (Slobodin, 1962: 63), that of the meat camp of 1938, households were arranged around a leader, presumably a man of wealth, according to gradations of wealth or poverty, but the group lacked the ingredient of sib membership. This fading of sibs as relevant in placements in gatherings is consistent with the general decline of sibs, as noted above.

Turning to considerations regarding the band, it should be noted that there was considerable interest in band societies during the 1960s, due largely to the writings of Julian H. Steward (1955) and Elman R. Service (1962). Steward posited three main types of band societies—the family level of integration, the patrilineal band, and the composite band. In referring to the northwestern Athaspaskans, he saw the composite band as the type in evidence, a type he describes as follows:

> The term "composite" is used to contrast the term "unilineal" to designate certain primitive societies which consist of many unrelated nuclear or biological families. These are integrated ... on the basis of constant association and co-operation rather than on the basis of kinship or alleged kinship. (Steward, 1955: 143)[2]

It would appear that Steward's characterization of Kutchin groupings is at variance with Slobodin's empirically derived picture. In the local group, the structure is based on primary bilateral kin ties. Also, in the trapping party, while some of the ties are of a more remote nature, behaviour appropriate to closer such kin is employed. Dick does not demonstrate comprehensiveness of kinship linkages on the larger group levels, but, contrary to Steward, he notes the importance of both unilineal (matrilinial) and cognatic descent in their structure. Steward (1955: 147) related an ecological basis for the large band found in the region as the communal hunting of large herds and migratory animals, while Slobodin (1962: 80) indicated that such animals had been hunted by groups of varying size. Service (1962: 87) agreed with Steward's designation of "composite" for the Athapaskans but rejected the notion of the total bands forming the hunting unit. He accounted for this departure from his prototypical patrilocal band on the basis of depopulation.[3] He also ignored the possibility of descent units among the northern Athapaskans. Another problem with Service's highly deductive formulation is his use of bifurcate merging terminology, whereas Slobodin demonstrated bifurcate collateral terms on the first ascending generation.

Another scheme of band level organization is offered by Helm (1968: 118–21) as based on her study of Mackenzie Dene to the east of the Peel River Kutchin. She denotes four types of groupings: the local band, the regional band, the task groups, and the tribe, which is characterized as "the greatest extension of population throughout which there is sufficient intermarriage to maintain many-sided social communication" (Helm, 1968: 118).[4] In comparing her characterization with Dick's, the closest correspondence comes with the Peel River local group and Helm's local band in both size and kinship composition. The main difference is that, while Helm's units form building blocks for larger units, the Peel River local groups are aberrant and isolated. This eliminates Helm's regional band, since it is built on the local bands. In function, her task groups might be similar to the trapping party and even the fish camps and meat camps of the Kutchin. However, Helm's groups are much smaller.

The appropriateness of the term of either *band* or *tribe* for the total Peel River population is perhaps moot. In terms of marriage practices one could argue for the tribe designation, considering that Slobodin (1962: 42) describes the total population as agamous; but he also notes (Slobodin, 1969a: 201) that "most marriages take place within the band, the next largest with the neighboring band and so on." Arguing for the band designation would be the existence of hereditary leadership over this large number of people (375) and the periodic assemblies. Indeed, for the Peel River people as a whole, Dick settles on the band designation, "for the politically autonomous community ... is more consonant with general usage for native North America (Kroeber, 1955: 303–305). The size of the Peel River community also conforms with Kroeber's suggestion of under 500 members for the band (Slobodin, 1962: 66).

In chapter 15 of *Band Organization of the Peel River Kutchin*, Dick discusses "variation" and "continuity." Under variation, he divided his discussion into recurrent or cyclic changes and non-recurrent or historical changes. For recurrent, the chief considerations were those of the seasonal faunal cycles, during which "the Peel River people combine and recombine into groups of varying sizes and function and stability" (78). Non-recurrent or historical changes to variations include those associated with the fur trade. These include the introduction of the breech-loading rifle, the use of dog teams and toboggans to increase the mobility needed to tend traplines in winter, and the use of imported fishnets. Dick also cites the effects of contacts with both whites and other Native people.

In dealing with the subject of continuity, Dick stressed uniformity over time of dependence on hunting, the uniformity of the habitat over time, as well as the occurrence of the same game animals, and when he was working on this study he recalled that the memory still existed of the mythology connected with various animals.

In summarizing the roles of variation and continuity in Peel River society and culture, Dick writes: "Peel River history to date has been characterized more by continuity or by variations around long-term norms than by drastic change" (1962: 84). That Dick found such changes that did occur could be accommodated by the Peel River people is clear from his concluding statement based on his 1938–39 and 1946–47 field research:

> Peel River social forms have manifested flexibility and have proved to be evidence of the adaptability of the Peel River people during this portion of their history (1900–47). This does not imply, however, that Peel River society is amorphous. It possesses a definite structure and this structure has shown viability and vitality. (1962: 86–87)

In the final section of *Band Organization of the Peel River Kutchin*, Dick (1962: 86–87) adds observations based on a 1961 field trip. During the interval between this study and the earlier ones, a number of important changes had taken place. These included the decline of the fur market, the introduction of trapline registration, petroleum exploration, the founding of Inuvik, work on a new road, and the expansion of welfare. These changes posed new challenges that would test the adaptability of the Peel River people.

NOTES

1 Dick (Slobodin, 1981: 530) notes that by the early 1970s the "practical ortho-graphic" Qwich'in had come into use. However, he continued to use Kutchin in his writings because "Kutchin has, at least for the present, been established in the literature" (Slobodin, 1994: 153).

2 The conception of the "composite" band of unrelated families is not an accurate portrayal of band-level societies, since it is extremely doubtful that the band exogamy that would be required exists. Such a condition has not been found in the literature on bands. Rather, the term "bilateral" is more accurate, since anthropologists of band societies have found kinship connections typifying the structures of bands. Making this assumption, which has been empirically determined in a number of cases, Helm (1969: 218–30) has devised a system of reckoning the sorts of kinship ties that pertain among members of bands.

3 Jenness (1922: 39) reports that for the eastern Copper Eskimo region the sort of depopulation situation described by Service occurred, presumably in the nineteenth century. If, indeed, this had occurred then, by the time of Rasmussen's visit to the region, in 1923–24, my reconstruction (Damas, 1969: 125) of his census (Ramussen, 1932: 71–80) shows that the band represented there

must have reconstituted itself into a unit showing extensive kinship connections rather than the compositeness that Service posed for such situations.

4 For an application of Helm's model with some terminological modifications for the Copper Eskimo, see Damas (1968). Closer to the Peel River region, McKennan (1969) found Helm's classification useful for interior Alaskan Athapaskans. Some agreement, in at least size, can be found in the report of the "Man the Hunter" conference" (Lee and DeVore, 1968), where a number of the participants found that the "magic numbers" of twenty-five and five hundred occurred in many of the band societies surveyed. These could be compared fairly well to Helm's local band and tribe.

References

Damas, David. 1969. Characteristics of Central Eskimo Band Structure. In David Damas, ed., *Contributions to Athropology: Band Societies*, 116–42. Ottawa: National Museum of Canada Bulletin No. 228.

——. 1972. "The Copper Eskimo." In M.G. Bicchieri, ed., *Hunters and Gatherers Today*, 3–5. New York: Holt, Rinehart and Winston.

Helm, June. 1968. "The Nature of Dgrib Socioterritorial Groups." In Richard B. Lee and Irven DeVore, eds., *Man the Hunter*, 118–25. Chicago: Aldine.

——. 1969. "A Method of Statistical Analysis of Primary Relative Bonds in Community Composition." In David Damas, ed., *Contributions to Anthropology: Band Societies*, 116–42. Ottawa: National Museum of Canada Bulletin No. 228.

Jenness, Diamond. 1922. *Report of the Canadian Arctic Expedition 1913–1918.* Vol. 12: *The Life of the Copper Eskimos*. Ottawa: F.A. Acland.

Kroeber, Alfred L. 1955. "Nature of the Land-Holding Group." *Ethnohistory* 2: 303–14.

Lee, Richard B., and Irven DeVore. 1968. *Man the Hunter*. Chicago: Aldin.

McClellan, Catherine. 1969. "Discussion." In David Damas, ed., *Contributions to Athropology: Band Societies*, 116–42. Ottawa: National Museum of Canada Bulletin No. 228.

McKennan, Robert A. 1969. "Athaspaskan Groupings and Social Organization." In David Damas, ed., *Contributions to Athropology: Band Societies*, 116–42. Ottawa: National Museum of Canada Bulletin No. 228.

Rasmussen, Knud. 1932. *Report of the Fifth Thule Expedition, 1921–1924.* Vol. 9: *Intellectual Culture of the Copper Eskimos*. Copenhagen: Gyldendalske Boghandel.

Service, Elman R. 1962. *Primitive Social Organization*. New York: Random House.

Slobodin, Richard. 1962. *Band Organization of the Peel River Kutchin*. National Museum of Canada Bulletin No. 179. Ottawa: Northern Affairs and National Resources.

——. 1969a. "Leadership and Participation in a Kutchin Trapping Party." In David Damas, ed., *Contributions to Anthropology: Band Societies*, 56–89. Ottawa: National Museum of Canada Bulletin No. 228.

——. 1969b. "Criteria for the Identification of Bands." In David Damas, ed., *Contributions to Anthropology: Band Societies*, 191–96. Ottawa: National Museum of Canada Bulletin No. 228.

——. 1981. "Kutchin." In June Helm, ed., *Handbook of North American Indi-ans*. Vol. 6: *The Subarctic*, 514–32. Washington, DC: Smithsonian Institu-tion.

——. 1994. "Kutchin Concepts of Reincarnation." In Antonia Mills and Richard Slobodin, eds., *Amerindian Rebirth: Concepts of Reincarnation among North American Indians and Inuit*, 136–55. Toronto: University of Toronto Press.

Steward, Julian H. 1955. *Theory of Change*. Urbana: University of Illinois Press.

CHAPTER NINE

Caribou Hunt

Richard Slobodin

AUTHOR'S NOTE

Recently, while going through some old files, I came across this piece of writing. It was composed and typed in November 1938, in the cabin occupied by Bob Fuller and me from September 1938 to May 1939. The Hudson's Bay Company post manager, Harry Ambrose, of Aberdeen, Scotland, had lent me a typewriter. I was to return to Fort McPherson from 1946 to '47 and for shorter visits in later years.

After writing the story, I sent it off to a magazine in the States. I must say that did not receive a rejection slip. I received no acknowledgement at all. The carbon copy I have just discovered has been resting for fifty-four and a half years in many and various residences and storage places.

On rereading the piece after all these years, I am struck by three thoughts. First, it is entirely true. I wrote it just after my return from the trip described, when the details were vivid in my mind. Later, I took part in longer and in some ways more eventful cross-country trips, but this was the first. Second, how nice everyone was. They really were. Cliff and Harry were first-rate companions, easygoing and tolerant of my ignorance and lack of skill. Carl Betz and Macauley were pleasant guys. Andrew Kunnizzi was remarkably generous in lending me a dog team, toboggan, and harness. In later years he continued to be helpful. Abe Stewart, James Simon, and Chief Julius were very fine men. As for Mrs. James (Sarah) Simon, I am glad to say that at the age of ninety she is still a dear friend.

The five last-named persons were or are members of the Peel River Kutchin band. My high opinion of Knud Lang, whom I came to know better in later years, is expressed in the dedication to him of Metis of the Mackenzie District. None of these people had ever heard of me before September 1938, when Fuller and I arrived by canoe.

The third thought: how young we were!

June 1993

From the cabin, where I was baking biscuits, I could hear Cliff Hagen calling, "Whoa there, Rock," to his lead dog as he stopped by the woodpile to speak with Bob. A moment later, as his tall form doubled through the doorway, Cliff was asking me, "Are you ready to leave early tomorrow? The Blake boys and Edward Idzé say there's caribou within a few miles of 'Klavik."

I could very well get ready. For a week we had been waiting for confirmation of the glad tidings that the big caribou herd had come over the mountains, over the divide from the Yukon side into the hills west of our Mackenzie delta country. Last year, and the year before that, there had been no meat until dangerously late in the winter, and, at that, hunters from the lower Mackenzie had had to go halfway to Dawson City to find them. Five hundred miles over mountains and through bush is a long distance to hunt and haul meat by dogsled. I was to learn that half that distance was no jaunt.

Until late that night, we were baking biscuits, cooking beans and dried fruit, and pulling ourselves together for the trip. By seven in the morning, hours before daylight, we were off down the frozen Peel River.

Since I was a beginner in dog-running, Cliff was doing the driving at first, hopping on and off of the tailboard of his toboggan. I jogged the first twelve miles, keeping just ahead of the dogs. By then, dawn was breaking, and so was my left foot, which I had turned on some rough ice.

In the wan daylight of Arctic November, we took turns driving until we reached a Loucheux[1] Indian camp at the Cut-Off, twenty miles from home. Driving the dogs along a well-travelled level trail proved ridiculously easy, and I took to wondering where this had been all my life. I was to find out later.

Along a river trail, dog-driving consists chiefly in standing on the tailboard, occasionally barking "Arrgh!" at the dogs to remind them that a superior creature keeps their destiny in hand. When the driver is feeling gracious, he may chirrup to the dogs or yodel at them. They like this.

At the Cut-Off, we had tea in the tent of Mrs. James Simon, a pleasant Indian lady of distinguished appearance. Her husband was up the Rat River at the time, searching for caribou.

When one is travelling in the North, summer or winter, every meal eaten, whether in the bush or at someone's camp, is known as "having tea." Perhaps this is because one does have tea, quarts of it. Dog-running in Arctic weather is dry work, and one certainly grows to look forward to a drink. When a native goes on a hunt, he takes a rifle, ammunition, tea, and an axe; then, if he can afford them, flour, sugar, lard, and an eider-down sleeping bag.

We had our troubles travelling after dark. We missed a portage that would have saved us a good many miles to Andrew Kunizzi's cabin, where we planned to spend the night. While we were looking for the portage entrance, Cliff and I became separated. After wallowing along the river through deep snow for what seemed an age of darkness, I built a fire and settled down to wait for Cliff to find me. This he did, after an hour or so.

Reunited, Cliff and I still could not find Andrew's cabin. We resigned ourselves to bush camp for the night, and were casting about for a good spot on which to build a fire shelter, when we caught sight of a large pile of eight-foot logs. Three minutes later we were pulling into Andrew's place amid the eager chatter of his fourteen dogs.

As we settled down to a "tea" served by the eldest daughters of the house, Cliff observed, "Fifty-five miles isn't a bad day's pull for four dogs on a new toboggan. And they aren't tired yet. Why, we could have gone another ten miles easy."

"Well, why didn't you, and bother somebody else—save me trouble?" our host retored. "I've got nothing fit for guests."

Andrew was kidding, of course. Hospitality is a prime virtue in the North, upon which all pride themselves. The jesting showed, however, a characteristic quality of the man.

Andrew Kunizzi is one of the three councilors of the Peel River Loucheux. A careful, intelligent man who generally knows what he is about, Andrew would be a moderately successful bourgeois is almost any society. Probably he would retain, in any other culture, his cautious tendency to disparage in public his own possessions and enterprises. In this he resembles many a businessman who would always reply gloomily to the question "How's business?" no matter how well his affairs were thriving.

While we were unhitching and feeding Cliff's dogs, we noticed on the Kunizzi fish stage a small mountain of frozen loche, a huge and voracious southern fish used for dog feed in these parts. When we returned to the cabin, Cliff complimented Andrew on his abundant supply of dog feed.

"Oh, I got a few fish. The loche aren't like two or three years ago, though," Andrew observed gloomily, "and fourteen dogs eat a lot of fish in a year."

In no way do I mean to imply that Andrew is stingy, a miser. I should be an utter ingrate to do so, since I was the fortunate recipient of a loan from him of four fine dogs and a toboggan, which I used for ten days.

After supper, Andrew remarked that it was inconvenient, travelling without dogs. I heartily agreed, and stated that, if I were staying in the country for any longer than one winter, I should try by all means to acquire a team. It would hardly be worthwhile for just a few trips, though.

"A man night borrow a team sometime," Andrew observed vaguely, stirring his tea.

Cliff and I said nothing, being privately of the opinion that this was very unlikely, especially when everyone was setting out after caribou. As I lay on the floor in my sleeping bag, however, I turned over Andrew's remark in my mind, and it seemed to grow in significance. The councilor would not expressly offer me a dog team, but this might be a hint that I could ask for one.

At breakfast, I put it to our host. "Will you lend me a team and a toboggan, Andrew?"

"Why, yes, I will," he replied. "Why not?"

As he hitched up four dogs for my use, Andrew complained, "Most of my dogs are young. They don't know how to work yet, and if they see game, they go crazy. Three of these I'm giving you are older dogs, though, and this bitch Flossie is not too bad."

Fervently I thanked Andrew and gave my toboggan the starting jerk: "Come on, you!"

Across two ponds, over a short trail, and onto a broad lake. Whee! This was the way to travel! Ahead of me, Cliff was yodeling to his team. At the end of the lake the trail led up to a gentle slope between young willows. Cliff shouted "Whoa!" as our teams came out onto a high bank overlooking a river. The portage trail had led us back to the Peel Channel. A quarter of a mile down the channel, the cabin of Carl Betz was visible.

Cliff, standing at the head of his toboggan, brought his team slowly over the crest of the bank. Holding taut the head rope, he eased the toboggan down the bank, and was away on the river without trouble. Doubtfully, I ordered my dogs forward. Before I could stop them they had trotted briskly over the bank, and the toboggan and I were plunging downhill on top of them, rolling over and over. At the bottom I pulled myself out of the snow, righted the toboggan, and, removing my mitts, set to work painfully untangling the harness traces.

Above me someone with a German accent asked, "What's the matter with them dogs?" The questioner was a short, grizzled, blue-eyed man standing beside a smoked-fish rack.

Abashed, I had to confess to what was quite apparent: the fault lay with the driver, not the dogs.

Carl Betz left his fish rack and joined Cliff and me at his cabin.

"You saw that Dick's got Andrew's dogs," Cliff remarked. "Do you know what? Andrew lent them to him. First time I've ever heard of a man lending a dog team in this country."

"That is good of Andrew," Carl agreed. "It's very unusual between an Indian and a white man. They're about his best dogs, too. Three of them are leaders."

"And Carl knows dogs," Cliff told me. "He breeds them."

Before we left Carl, Cliff bought a dog from him. Like most Artic purchases, this was to be paid for in the spring, after the trapping and ratting seasons.

We made very poor time that day, becoming involved among some inland lakes on a long portage. A winter portage is a shortcut across country where the river trail makes a wide sweeping bend. An average winter portage involves going up a steep bank, along a narrow path among trees, across the bumpy surface of a frozen muskeg swamp, over several lakes, and through more muskeg and bush before slamming down another steep bank onto the level river trail again.

There is little or no compromise about the approach to a portage. You are skimming along a smooth river, lolling in the carryall of your toboggan or standing on the tailboard, the head rope slack in your hand, chirruping to your dogs occasionally. Suddenly the trail makes a right-angle turn in the horizontal plane—towards the bank—and another right-angle bend in the vertical plane—up the bank. Up the bank, no matter how steep that bank may be, means straight up. Seldom is a portage entrance on the slant.

You hop off of the tailboard, or jump out of the carryall; you seize the handlebars of your toboggan, put your head down, and shove, shouting incisive exhortation to the dogs. If the team stops partway up, you must go to the head of the toboggan, grasp the wheel dog's traces, or the front ground lashings, and pull with everything you've got, to give the sled a start. At the same time you bark or scream at your dogs—according to your nature—hoping to get them to buck into their collars just as you start the lead. If they do so, you advance for a few feet. If not, you will probably lose ground. Eventually your dogs reach the level, your toboggan goes over the hump, and you, still on the hill, hold fast to the long head rope, letting the dogs pull you up the rest of the slope. You feel that you've earned this much consideration from them.

We stopped at Old Man Harrison's fox ranch at three o'clock and decided to stay for the night. Harrison told us we were now eleven miles from Andrew Kunizzi's.

"Good gravy!" Cliff cried. "Fifty-seven miles with four dogs yesterday, and today only eleven miles with nine dogs!"

We considered re-hitching the dogs and continuing to Knud Lang's cabin, twenty miles farther north. Later that evening we were glad we did not do so, for Henry Harrison dropped in, just back from killing caribou. Harry was no longer living at the fox ranch with his father and sisters, but he supplied them with meat.

Harry brought us the news for which we had been looking all along: the caribou were this side of Aklavik.

"They're up the Husky and the Willow," he told us. "I want to hunt again, but I have to look at my trapline first, so if you fellows can stop at Macauley's cabin tomorrow, I'll meet you there on the morning after."

Thus it was agreed. The next morning was clear and snapping cold. As we bowled along the channel trail, frost flakes fell from a clear pale-blue sky. Sunlight turned them into golden spangles; if the air was like wine, these motes made it *Goldwasser.*

Cliff, standing on his tailboard just ahead of my lead dog's nose, turned around and sat on the lazy-back, facing me.

"I want to tell you about this fellow Macauley, Dick," he began. "Mac's not a bad fellow, but he and I are sort of rivals, and he sure hates to see me get ahead of him in anything. How would it be if I told him you were a millionaire's son from the States and that you're paying me ten bucks a day to take you hunting? Boy, that'd make old Mac green!"

"Well, okay, Cliff—as long as it doesn't cost me anything. Which reminds me: How, if the matter comes up, are you going to account for the fact that I haven't got much money with me?" That morning I had spent most of the cash I had brought along on dog food from Old Man Harrison.

"Well, I can tell him or anyone else that you get just a certain allowance from home."

"Yes. Look, a couple of years ago I lost $100,000 in two nights at Monte Carlo. Ever since then my father sends me only a few dollars' pocket money, paying all my bills directly."

"That's great! Won't I hand it to old Mac!"

Mac proved to be a stout, comfortable-looking, rather genial person. I had heard he was a good cook, and there was that about his appearance, and in the neatness of his cabin, which presaged a good supper. While we were eating it, Mac stepped outside to fetch in some wood.

Cliff leaned over and whispered, "He sure looked sick when I told him."

That evening we talked until very late, discussing politics and swapping yarns. Mac told us of experiences along the Arctic coast, and I narrated adventures that seemed appropriate for a footloose scion of wealth, slightly incognito.

I shall always hope that one story, at least, that Mac told was less fictional than were mine. This tale concerned his manufacture of an "Eskimo idol" and of its acquisition by a Catholic priest bound for Rome. Mac had reason to believe that it might be now reposing in the Vatican Museum.

In the morning we were half-awakened by the barking of the dogs, but none of us stirred from his sleeping bag. Forty minutes later, Harry breezed in, lit the fire, and set water on for tea.

"I camped at Lang's last night. Heard your dogs barking when I started off for here."

Lang's cabin is five miles from Mac's. A lifetime spent in the open had given Harry and the dogs acute hearing. Harry's father, fox farmer Harrison, was born in Milwaukee; his mother was a Dogrib Indian. Harry was born in a tent on the Barren Lands, northeast of Great Bear Lake. Now, at twenty-one, Harry ranks high in the Mackenzie delta as an industrious trapper and hunter.

That morning, where the Husky River joins the Peel Channel, twelve miles from Aklavik, we turned off the channel trail. Here was an encampment of Slavey Indians from Fort Good Hope. Thad, at whose cabin we stopped for a moment, had been hurrying away to track a wolverine that had made off with a trap on one foot, but he stopped to tell us of an experience he once had after shooting a caribou.

"I wounded a pretty big bull," That said. "When I went up to cut his throat, he got to his feet and started to walk slowly away. You know how they do: walk away and lie down, walk away and lie down again. I didn't want to have to chase him for miles and then haul him all the way back, so I made a quick run and grabbed his horns, twisting his head to throw him. But the old bastard jerked his head up, and the next thing I knew, I was lying across his back and he was away."

"Christ, you ought to have seen Thad bouncing along on that bull!" his partner Joe interposed. "He kept reaching around the caribou's neck, sawing away at the throat with his knife."

"Well, I got him, all right. Now I got to get that damned wolverine. Joe'll fix you some tea, boys."

It speaks highly for our enterprise that we did not stop for tea this time, though we had gone all of seven miles that morning.

That night we sat around a table in the Coalmine Cabin, far up the Willow River.

"I'd sure like to try Thad's trick," Cliff said. "Bulldog one of them wounded buggers, or ride him."

"You're the man for it," we agreed. "After all, a caribou ought to be easy for a fellow that's been a cowboy and ridden in rodeos."

"It'll make a good picture for you to take," Cliff observed to me.

Evenings are long on the trail in winter. Unless one is forced to travel late, one usually plans to camp by 4 p.m. Cutting wood, getting water, starting a fire, and preparing supper for man and dogs takes no more than two hours. There is no point in going to bed immediately, as one is not likely to start off before eight o'clock on the following morning.

Not a man of us had thought to bring playing cards. Cliff and Henry play the guitar, but a person who intends to haul meat for hundreds of miles does not carry guitars to take up space in his carryall.

We told stories of travel. Cliff and I exchanged information on beating one's way by freight, and conveyed the fine points of hitchhiking to Harry, who has never been south of Great Bear Lake.

One of us struck up a song, then another followed suit. As we grew more animated, Cliff began to tap on a kettle. Harry and I arranged some tin cans as musical glasses. Cliff broke into a cowboy yodel, and in a moment his moccasined feet were stamping the Red River jig. As Harry and I did some inspired work with tins and pots, the dogs joined in. Most sled dogs have a remarkable ear for musical pitch, and, in their quite unmournful howling, can create some fine harmony. Soon they were sending in style, with Cliff interpolating hot licks.

In the midst of the caterwauling within the cabin and outside, some of the dogs broke into frenzied barking. We hurried out. A short search revealed fresh bear signs on the river ice, fifty yards from the cabin. From the tracks it was evident that the animal, moseying along on his ursine business, had been badly frightened by the unscheduled jam session. He has probably lived a better life ever since.

On the following day we met with the toughest going that I had as yet encountered. This was, specifically, in the middle of the day's journey, when we climbed a three-mile slope, many sections of which were as steep as some rather bad portage entrances—only instead of being twenty or thirty feet long, these stretches extended for hundreds of feet. My companions, having larger teams and being better drivers than I, left me far behind on this slope.

One hellish section of the hill will always stand out in memory as a grade-A blot. I see the dogs turn to the left as they start up the head-wall of a very narrow draw, so narrow that the eight-foot toboggan cannot turn crosswise in it. Shouting and cracking my head rope, I painfully lift the back end of the toboggan around, hauling it over boulders, breaking down small willows, stumbling, sweating, and cursing. We start up the head-wall through a thick growth of dwarf willows. For every step I must either shove from behind, my shoulder against the lazy-back of the sled, or get in front and pull on the head rope. When we have advanced clear of the willows, the going becomes worse, because there is less purchase for the feet. Here, whenever I strain against the toboggan, I begin to lose footing and the team and sled slide backward a yard or so.

The dogs whine, as working dogs will when they find themselves unable to do as they are ordered. I step right in front of the toboggan head, between the traces of Tommy, the Coppermine husky wheel dog, and I grasp these traces. Brand, the lead dog, is stretching his forepaws ahead, digging his claws into the hard snow in an effort to draw himself forward. We get to work all together: "Come on, boys! Go!"

We move. I hop out of the traces and pull on the toboggan head. Brand reaches the top of the head-wall, finds himself on a gentler slope. That's all we need. He'll get us up now.

At the top of the three-mile slope, a long rest was enjoyed by all. From there one could see almost the entire delta, shiny with creeks and channels. To the northeast were the Caribou Hills, beyond which lay the Reindeer Station. Almost due north was Shingle Point, on the shore of the Arctic Ocean. Along the Peel Channel, seven dog teams were hurrying to Aklavik. After caribou news, no doubt.

Mac's tent, which we slept in that night, was barely large enough for the stove and our three sleeping bags, spread over caribou skins. There was no jam session. Lying in his bedding, with the prospect of remaining there for twelve or thirteen hours, Cliff was moved to ask, "How about a ghost story, Dick?"

I related, as well as I could remember them, W.W. Jacobs's "The Monkey's Paw" and Michael Arlen's "The Gentleman from America." The storytelling had the desired effect: my listeners dropped off gently during the second narrative.

While scouting, after they had arrived at camp, Cliff and Harry had seen hundreds of caribou in another valley, over the next ridge. Next morning it was determined that we strike camp and move five miles up John Warton's Creek, to be nearer the hunting. Harry emptied the stove, loaded it, the stovepipe, and the tent onto his toboggan, and we drove up to a well-sheltered spot, near plenty of dead dry willows. We pitched the tent and chained our dogs with particular care, lest they sight caribou. Taking up our .30-.30s, boxes of shells, and hunting knives, we set off afoot over the next ridge.

Soon we were picking our way over a terrain consisting of nothing but large and slippery boulders, trying to avoid holes, carrying our rifles more or less in our teeth. I thought of Wolfe's troops crawling up to the Plains of Abraham and wondered if they had been fortunate enough to possess bandoliers.

In the next valley we had a sweeping view of miles of Alpine-type snowfields but no view of caribou. Evidently the deer were on the move toward the south. Where they had been thick the day before, not one was to be found. As we tramped across the valley toward a higher ridge, Cliff and Harry decided to divide forces for scouting purposes. Harry was to go straight over the ridge, forward for a while, and then to the left, or southward. Cliff and I were to go south down this valley for a few miles and then over the ridge.

"What'll the signals be when we see each other, Harry? Let's see. Hold your rifle straight up over your head if you want the other fellow to come."

"All right. And wave the gun to mean he should keep going."

Cliff and I plodded along the valley, following a single caribou's tracks. But we were following them backward. The animal had been headed in the opposite direction. I wondered why it should concern us whence the caribou was coming.

When I asked Cliff about this, he pointed out a large canine spoor about twenty feet to one side of the deer track.

"Wolf chased this caribou," he observed. "He probably met a bunch of them somewhere and picked out one to chase. The rest of the bunch naturally buggered off somewheres else."

This interpretation proved to be correct. After an hour or so, the trail led to the foot of the ridge, and there we saw where it had broken away from a veritable maelstrom of caribou tracks. It was here that the wolf tracks came up to the caribou. The rest of the band had evidently milled around, turned, and gone over the ridge at this point.

Heartened and excited, we worked our way up the slippery caribou road. We hadn't advanced far on the plateau above when we caught sight of Harry. Sure enough, he was holding his rifle motionless overhead.

Ten minutes later we were with him.

"They just moved down this valley, around the bend to the right," Harry told us. "Just as I came over that little rise back there, I saw them moving off. A big bull came right up to the rock I was lying behind. I couldn't have missed him, but if I'd have shot, they would all have beat it, and then there'd be no hunting for anybody else."

"We've got to move fast now," Cliff stated. "Let's go!"

After we had trotted for fifteen or twenty minutes there came hoarse whisper from Cliff:

"There they are!"

Two miles down a wide valley was a large cluster of dots, with other dots sprinkled around. We paused.

"God damn it," Harry whispered. "No cover at all."

"Christ, no," Cliff whispered. "Doesn't seem to be any way of getting up on them, though we're downwind. Unless one or two of us goes across this valley, circles around that mountain, and comes out ahead of them to drive them back this way."

"But, hell, that'd take till 'way after dark."

"I know," Cliff agreed gloomily, "but now that I see meat I'm not leaving without some."

At this impasse, the greenhorn ventured a suggestion. "Look," I said, "see that belt of rocks about a third of a mile from the caribou? If we got there we wouldn't be seen, would we?"

"No, but how in hell to get there?"

"Well, maybe we could crouch down low and—"

"By God!" Cliff cried, forgetting to whisper. "That gives me an idea. We'll try something like the old Eskimo trick. Give me your gun, Harry. Now look, I'll have these rifles crossed over my head like horns and you fellows crouch down right behind me and we'll run. It's supposed to have sort of the shape of a caribou coming toward you, from a distance."

We removed our mitts and twisted them behind us on their strings, to get them out of the way. We wanted to be ready to shoot at any time. Then off we went, jogging single file, Cliff in front with the guns over his head, Harry close behind him, and I crowding Harry from the rear.

The caribou didn't seem to mind us at all. As we drew nearer, they took on the semblance of the animals I had so often read about and of which I had seen pictures: standing about three feet high at the shoulder, with gray and brown hair, antlers projecting straight forward as they moved on slowly, heads down, peacefully cropping the moss under the snow.

When we got to within a hundred yards of the rocks, Cliff slammed Harry's gun into the latter's hands and broke into a sprint. Harry and I bounded after him. We had hardly crouched among the rocks when Cliff yelled, "Let 'em have it!"

Away we blazed.

The next ten minutes unreeled themselves as an old-fashioned movie, jerky and flickering, with the actors moving too fast. The flickers on the consciousness were the rifle shots exploding in irregular bursts around, above, and as it were, within each of us during that time. Kneeling within a space of two or three feet, we fired right past each other, and, as the caribou shifted, we fired across each other's bows. Harry's cheek was heated by the discharge from Cliff's gun. Harry, in turn was at one time practically resting his stock on my barrel while shooting at right angles to my line of fire.

The first six or eight shots seemed to have no effect on the caribou's health or morale. Then some deer must have been hit, for one could see the outlying caribou hurrying toward the main body of the herd. They were bunching at the attack, as I had often heard they did.

Firing into the mass of animals was a haphazard way of hunting, but it was all we could do at our three-hundred-yard range until the caribou, having apparently decided on a course of action, suddenly broke for every draw leading out of the valley.

A cow caribou swung and galloped right past our battery. This cow exerted a baneful influence on two calves and another cow. Here were four caribou—and of the tenderest meat—moving past within fifty yards. That was the kind of caribou shot one heard about!

Of the mothers and young going past us, one calf got away. Another bunch were going over a nearby hill, running hard. Cliff and Harry jumped up and took after them.

"I haven't any more shells," I shouted, glad of the excuse to refrain from running.

"Then cut a throat," Harry called back.

Having interpreted this to mean a caribou's throat, I was hacking at the dewlap of the larger cow when the others came back, considerably winded, to say that the caribou had outdistanced them.

"Well, anyway, we got meat," Cliff pointed out. "There's these three— four, five. And that bull over there! I knew that bastard was wounded."

Nearly half a mile away a rather large bull caribou had paused in his flight and was now circling slowly about with head lowered, apparently looking for a quiet place in which to lie down.

Cliff hurried off toward the bull. Harry set to work cleaning the larger cow. In three slashes he laid the throat bare to the spine. Then, unsheathing the hatchet he carried in a shoulder strap, he chopped at the back of the neck until the spine was smashed. He then seized the antlers and gave the head a sharp twist, pulling it loose completely.

"You sure can make good soup with caribou head," he stated, winking at me with a broad grin. "Now we pull out the guts."

In no time Harry had the belly slashed open and was pulling out intestines. He cursed blithely as some of them burst, covering his hands with filth.

"Even if you leave them for only overnight without gutting, the meat don't taste so good. Now that she's empty, she'll freeze nicely. You said you want the skin, Dick? Okay, watch me this time."

From the belly opening Harry made an incision in the skin, skirting the hindquarters. Slipping the blade of his large pocket knife under the skin, he began to work it loose from the flesh. When he had a handhold, he grasped the edge of the skin and pulled. In places, it was necessary to snip at it with the knife. Within five minutes Harry stood up, holding the skin at arm's length. We were admiring the short hair, thick-matted like the pile of a good carpet, when from down the valley we heard Cliff calling me. As we looked up, he beckoned.

The bull caribou was lying a short distance from the spot where it had first paused in flight. Cliff was some forty yards from it.

As I neared him, he called in a stage whisper, "Get your camera set and we'll try and make this good. I'm out to ride or throw the frogger. Suppose you stand where he can see you. Then he'll keep his eye on you and won't pay no mind to me."

I moved into the caribou's line of vision and walked slowly toward him. The bull heaved his shoulder up slightly and half raised his head. Meanwhile, in the background, Cliff was creeping along like a bird dog, his lanky form jack-knifed as he crouched, spine parallel to the ground. In his hand a case knife gleamed. The better to see, he had pushed his parka hood back, and his maroon-coloured beret sat askew on his tousled hair.

When he was quite close to the bull, he called softly, "Move again."

I raised the camera and stepped forward, hoping that the shutter had not frozen. At this, the caribou rolled and got his legs underneath him. He was beginning to rise on his haunches when Cliff dashed forward and lunged with his knife. But the caribou was no longer there.

Cliff swore. "I just nicked his ass. Oh, well, no use chasing him anymore today. We'll find him tomorrow, dead. He's got a slug through both lungs."

By the time the five caribou were gutted and drained, it was nearly dark. It was late when we got back to camp, at least twelve miles away. We were all dead tired, but after supper the boys wanted me to tell another story. This time it was "The Wendigo," a weird tale of the north by Algernon Blackwood.

"Wendigo?" Harry looked puzzled. "Oh, you mean like the Witigo—the bad spirit of the bush that the Indians from upriver, around Lake Athabasca, talk about."

As is often the case, the narrator enjoyed he storytelling perhaps more than the listeners did. Not only did it pass the time pleasantly, but it provided something that I could do for my companions. At twenty-three, I was the oldest member of the hunting party. But my partners, thoroughly at home in the bush or in the mountains, were continually helping me and doing things for me.

On the next day, the seventh day of the trip, we drove the dogs by a circuitous route to the scene of the hunting and hauled the caribou back to camp in the toboggans.

The wounded bull that Cliff had been chasing was lying near the gutted deer. His legs were stiff and were beginning to turn skyward as the stomach swelled. While Harry slammed at the rubbery belly with an axe, Cliff held a flaming stick near the point where the cut was to be made. He wanted to see whether he could ignite the gas that would rush out. The axe sank in and the gas whistled forth, blowing out the torch and nearly suffocating Cliff.

Guiding a heavily loaded toboggan over stretches of loose rock was rather a back-breaker. My toboggan insisted on falling over on one side continually, until Harry came back, unlashed the load, and readjusted it so it was properly balanced. Difficulties on the high ridges were to be expected, but I was considerably embittered on the following day, when, on coming to that long, bad slope that had given the team such trouble to climb, I found that it was almost as bad in the descent—not, as one might suppose, because of the danger in excessive speed but because it was a tough pull.

As Andrew's toboggan had no foot brake, Cliff had advised me to fasten three dog chains around it, to act as drags on the slope. Chains thus arranged are very powerful brakes, and Cliff knew that two of them would be plenty, but he wanted to make sure that no accident befell the team or toboggan.

However, the four dogs could barely budge the heavy load with three chains on. Cursing and pulling at the head rope every two feet, having the dogs stop and whine—this was bad enough on an uphill grade, but it was particularly exasperating when we were pointed downhill at a steep angle. I painfully removed one chain, and then another, and we began to go.

When we hit the trail through the willows, the dogs felt better. The toboggan had a crazy ride, bouncing off of every other sapling and sliding sideways on fallen logs.

The next morning, as we left the Coalmine Cabin, it was really cold. The dogs could hardly stand still while we were lashing our bedrolls and grub sacks into the carryalls.

"There always seems to be a damned headwind in this canyon," Harry said, "and now with this cold weather, look out you don't freeze your face."

Running behind the dogs warmed most of the body, but it did not help certain vital spots. Soon Cliff, Harry, and I were standing on the tailboards of our toboggans, each of us with one mitt covering his nose and the other pressed against his crotch, keeping balance on the swaying vehicle as well as possible.

We remained in this position for about ten miles, until the pageant was interrupted by a portage. Running over some frozen muskeg, we reached the crossing of a lake two miles wide. Here the wind died away and we relaxed into the lazy-backs, sitting with our backs to the dogs and admiring the mountains from which we were now emerging.

The terrain was such as one sees in California: a plateau stretching flat up to sudden mountains. Those crinkled white steeps behind us already towered remote and inaccessible, guardians of some inviolable Shangri-La. No longer could one believe that, two days before, we had been with the dog teams fifty miles inside the mountain mass, among pinnacles higher and wilder than these outward ramparts.

Late in the day we reached the Slavey encampment. At our first view of the Peel Channel from the top of the bank, we noticed an alteration in the surface of the main trail. In the snow someone had written in huge letters, stamping them out with his snowshoes, the words "My sweetheart Adel." Adel, or Adele, was a girl in the Slavey camp.

Cliff dashed down the bank and wrote a brief footnote to this Arctic valentine.

Loaded as we were with our six caribou and two that Harry had left cached from his previous hunt, we found some of the portage entrances hard going. At many of them, the three of us would wrestle each toboggan up in turn, the driver pulling at the head and the other two braced against the back. If those at the back slackened for an instant, the dogs, toboggan, and driver all skidded downhill for yards. We dreaded the necessity of unpacking the loads and relaying them to the top. Fortunately we were never obliged to do so.

As we stopped for a smoke in the middle of a lake, Cliff remarked, "About a mile to Lang's."

"Do you suppose he's back from his eastern trapline?"

"Yep," Harry said, "he's just starting a fire in his cabin."

"How in hell do you know that?"

"I smell the smoke."

Lang's cabin was almost warm when we arrived. As we carried our sleeping bags inside, Lang set some preserved eggs out to thaw and fished some frankfurters out of a brine barrel.

"I found these in my nets the other day," he told us. "They seem to be saltwater creatures."

"That museum you're always sending specimens to," Harry said, "send them one of these."

While our host skinned a cross fox, he told us that the main herd of caribou, numbering in the tens of thousands, had moved south to the valley of the Rat, less than two days from McPherson. All of the Peel River Indians were out hunting. The news had come just after we had turned into the mountains.

"We'll hunt again," Harry declared. "I'll look at my traps and nets and then meet you fellows at McPherson."

That night I returned Andrew's dogs and toboggan, leaving Andrew three-quarters of a caribou. He was away hunting, and his daughters planned to go up the Rat after him, to help haul meat back, as soon as the dogs had had a day's rest.

At Carl Betz's, we left Harry. He was to bring the rest of my load up to McPherson when he came on the following week.

We got a very late start the next day—the eleventh of our trip. As I had to walk the thirty miles to the Cut-Off, most of it after dark and in deep drifts without benefit of snowshoes, I was happy to settle down in the Simons's warm tent with a plate of spareribs before me.

All of the men living at the Cut-Off were home from hunting, with many caribou and more cached in the hills. Several of them were going up to McPherson on the morrow to sell meat.

"This man," James Simon told me, "promised himself to give you a ride to the Fort tomorrow. He's got six dogs."

"Who, me?" asked Abe Stewart. "Let's see. My load will be twenty-two quarters, and Dick makes twenty-six, if he's all there."

It was, we learned, Sunday night, and, since James Simon was the lay preacher or catechist of the encampment, there were evening services in his tent. Mrs. Simon set some candles on pointed sticks, which were stuck upright between some of the thin, straight willow branches that overlay the spruce-bough floor. James opened the Loucheux Book of Common Prayer, and one of his girls went outside and rang a handbell. Soon everyone in camp was seated in the tent. Next to James sat bulky Chief Julius, hereditary and elected headman of the Peel River people. From an embroidered case he drew a pair of gold-rimmed spectacles. After donning them, he followed the prayers devoutly.

Cliff and I lay in a corner, trying not to appear more comfortable than was fitting at a religious exercise. It was no use. As I lolled on a mountain sheep's skin covered with heavy wool, my head pillowed on an eiderdown sleeping robe, the soothing drone of prayer and hymn-singing in a foreign tongue soon put me to sleep.

"Most comfortable prayer meetin' ever I was at," Cliff pronounced when it was over.

Next morning, Abe and his dogs didn't seem very happy about the added weight on his toboggan, so after a few miles I took to running. Chief Julius was just behind me. After I had run about half a mile, the chief whistled and called out in Loucheux to Abe.

"Old chief wants you to ride with him," Abe told me.

Julius has arthritis and cannot run very much, but he has seven excellent dogs and his sled is a limousine among toboggans, so he seldom finds it necessary to step off of his tailboard. He motioned me to straddle the load in his carryall and away we went. For the most part the trail was on level glare ice, though from time to time we slammed violently over shelves of piled drift ice. Once or twice I fell off of the load, much to Julius's amusement.

Ahead of us, Cliff was singing to his dogs, cracking his whip. I tried a song or two, and the chief's music-loving dogs seemed to speed up, perhaps in an effort to get away from me.

"Fine," said the chief. "You sing. Make dogs go good."

It occurred to me to try songs that were as incongruous to the situation as possible, so I could feel that never before had they been sung under such circumstances, nor would they ever be again. "The Kashmiri Love Song," "Bei Mir Bist Du Schoen," "One Big Union for Two," "The Dirty Little Coward Who Killed Mr. Howard"—these and others were trolled forth.

The chief began to punctuate the musical phrases with cracks of his whip, chirruping and shouts of encouragement—to the dogs or me.

"Wahoo!" he yelled.

"What was that?" I cried, astonished.

"Keep singing. Go ahead," Julius exhorted.

After a few more bars it came again, almost a yodel, consisting as it did of a low, guttural "Wa" and a long-drawn, high-pitched "hoo-oo-oo!"

We were quite pleased with ourselves, the nine of us—the dogs oping easily, I caroling, for better for worse, and the chief wahooing at the end of each measure.

When we reached the Fort, Julius went off to his own cabin, but Abe, Cliff, and James stayed at our place for the night. As they sat at supper, with Bob and me, I asked, "Does the chief ever read the comics?"

"Naw," replied Abe. "He can't read, not even Loucheux. These specs you saw on him last night are just for show."

AFTERWORD

Reading this piece again after more than half a century, I'm impressed with its realism and truthfulness. But reality and truth can be viewed from various angles. This is a snapshot of reality from the viewpoint of a very young man who had plunged into a world and way of life completely exotic to him, but one to which he was determined to adjust.

Of course this picture is only a tiny fragment of the natural scene and of the lives encountered. In later years I learned much more about these people and others, and also about the wonderful country.

What happened to the cast of characters?

CARL BETZ AND MACAULEY. I visited Betz a couple of times later but never met Macauley again. One of the most striking things about Macauley was that he had been a concert pianist in western Canada. Difficult to believe, but he proved it with clippings, photographs, and old concert programs extracted from a dusty steamer trunk. His transition to Arctic trapper must have been quite a story, but I do not know it.

ANDREW KUNNIZZI. Andrew became a good friend and to some extent an informant in my later research. His son Isaac was a promising graphic artist, but in the circumstances of that time was unable to pursue that career. He was a trapper.

ABRAHAM STEWART. One of the most popular members of the Peel River band. Died of tuberculosis during World War II.

JULIUS MARTIN. The last direct hereditary chief of the Tetlit Gwich'in (Peel River Kutchin band) and a member of a descent group from which the chiefs had been chosen since pre-contact times. A genial man and a conscientious leader to the extent that he could be. He died, well up in years, in 1949.

JAMES SIMON. Also a member of the chiefly descent group. An active trapper, he eventually became an ordained Anglican priest. Certainly one of the finest persons, of any ethnicity, that I have ever known. He died in the 1970s.

SARAH SIMON. To some extent Metis but a band member. An extremely fine, kind, and thoughtful person, as well as very devout. The Simons were a devoted couple. None of their own children survived past early years, but they adopted several, including a Metis girl who was largely white and an Inuit girl. Their home was always open to visitors. In 1992 Sarah was inducted into the Order of Canada, principally for her work in the translation of religious texts.

KNUT LANG (1895–1964). Danish in origin, a trapper and small-scale trader in the Mackenzie delta since the mid-1920s. He had little formal education but made of himself a man of learning by means of reading and intelligent observation. He was in fact a corresponding member of two learned societies. In the course of many visits to his book-lined cabin, I read for the first time Will Durant's *The Story of Philosophy* and that fundamental classic of animal ecology *Voles, Mice and Lemmings*, by Charles Elton. Universally respected, Lang was for years an elected member of the Northwest Territories Council.

CLIFF HAGEN. Twenty-two years old in 1938, a former cowpuncher and rodeo rider from northern British Columbia. When we went hunting together, he was newly married to the former Margaret MacDonald, the beautiful Metis granddaughter of John Firth, legendary Hudson's Bay Company chief factor. Cliff and I met almost by accident at Old Crow, Yukon, in the summer of 1977. Both of us were a lot less carefree than we had been thirty-nine years earlier. In the intervening years, Cliff told me, he had become a heavy drinker and because of this had lost Margaret and their children. By 1977 he did not drink at all and greatly missed his family. But he was able to take pride in the accomplishments of his offspring.

HARRY HARRISON. Twenty-one years old in 1938. We met at Inuvik, Northwest Territories, in the summer of 1977. Harry was one of the most successful trappers in the region and among the most persistent in maintaining a life in the bush. When he was young, he fell in love with a girl of the Peel River band. As Harry was Roman Catholic and all of the Peel River people, certainly at that time, were strongly Anglican, marriage was impossible. Harry was embittered by this, but eventually he married an Inuit girl who proved to be a good wife and mother. Harry's sisters, whom I knew well, told me how he had remained solicitous of their welfare through the years. Harry is a man upon whom one may rely.

BOB FULLER. Twenty-five years old in 1938. Offstage in this narrative but the principal figure in our year-and-a-half-long northern trip. Fuller—he was, as he said, Bob to acquaintances, Fuller to friends—was a woodcarver and designer, and as good with his mind as he was with his hands. We remained friends pretty well until his untimely death in San Francisco in the 1970s.

DICK SLOBODIN. I've lost track of him.

NOTE

1 Loucheux is an old-fashioned name for the Kutchin or Gwich'in people of the western subarctic.

RICHARD SLOBODIN BIBLIOGRAPHY

Note: The following list does not include the approximately twenty book reviews.

1998. *Rivers: As Seen in "Regeneration."* Stroud: Alan Sutton Publishing. [First published as part of Slobodin 1978, below, this 85-page book tied in with the film *Regeneration.* In the film, Dr. William Rivers, the subject of Slobodin's biography, features due to his association with Siegfried Sassoon and Robert Graves at Craiglockhart War Hospital.]

1994. (with Antonia Mills), eds. *Amerindian Rebirth: Reincarnation Belief among North American Indians and Inuit.* Toronto: University of Toronto Press.

1992. A Search for Authenticity. Ms.

1989. "Follow the Drinking Gourd." *Northern Review* 3–4:42–53.9.

1988. Norsemen. Unpublished ms. 20 pp.

1985. "Tell Him I'm Gone." *Ta Panta* [McMaster University] 2, no. 1: 2–7.

1982. Review of Hiroka Sue Hara, *The Hare Indians and Their World. Canadian Journal of Native Studies.*

1981. "Alexander Hunter Murray and Kutchin Hair Style." *Arctic Anthropology* 18, no. 2: 29–42.

1981. "Kutchin." In *Handbook of North American Indians,* Vol. 6: The Subarctic, ed. June Helm. Washington: Smithsonian Institution.

1981. "Subarctic Metis." In *Handbook of North American Indians,* Vol. 6: The Subarctic, ed. June Helm. Washington: Smithsonian Institution.

1981. "Views of W.H.R. Rivers." *American Anthropologist* 83: 397–98.

1980. "Some Recent Developments in Subarctic Culture History and Ethnohistory: Comments." *Arctic Anthropology* 17, no. 2: 52–59.

1979. "'Welcome to Saskatoon': A Late-Depression Glimpse." *Saskatchewan History* 32, no. 2: 74–78.

1978. *W.H.R. Rivers.* New York: Columbia University Press.

1976. Early Friends: Mrs. Peters, the Rosicrucian, and Jane. *Journal of Anthropology at McMaster* 2: 1–8.

1976. "'The Fearful Curse': Lewis Carroll, Stammering, and the Hunt-Rivers Connection." *McMaster University Library Research News* 3, no. 4 (January).

1976. (with Joseph Sigman). "Stammering in the Dodgson Family: An Unpublished Letter by Lewis Carroll." *Victorian Newsletter* 49: 26–27.

1975. "Without Fire: A Kutchin Tale of Warfare, Survival, and Vengeance." In Proceedings of the Northern Athapaskan Conference, 1971, ed. A.M. Clark, pp. 260–301. Ottawa: National Museum of Man Mercury Series in Ethnology, Paper No. 27.1975. "Canadian Subarctic Athapaskans in the Literature to 1965." *Canadian Revue of Sociology and Anthropology* 12, no. 3: 278–89.

1975. "Northern Athapaskan Research: Some Comments." In Proceedings of the Northern Athapaskan Conference, 1971, ed. A. McFadden Clark, pp. 786–97. Ottawa: National Museum of Man Mercury Series in Ethnology, Paper No. 27.

1975. "Anthro at Mac." *Journal of Anthropology at McMaster* 1(Spring): 5–19.

1973. "Variation and Continuity in Kutchin Society." In *Cultural Ecology*, ed. Bruce Cox. Toronto: McClelland and Stewart.

1972. "'The Indians of Canada' Today: Questions on Identity." In *Canada: A Sociological Profile*, 2nd ed., ed. W.E. Mann. Toronto: Copp Clark.

1972. "The Metis of Northern Canada." In *The Blending of Races*, ed. N.P. Gist and A.G. Dworkin. New York: Wiley-Interscience.

1971. "Metis of the Far North." *In Minority Canadians 1: Native Peoples*, ed. J.L. Elliott. Scarborough, ON: Prentice Hall Canada.

1971. "The Chief Is a Man." *Western Canadian Journal of Anthropology* 2, no. 3: v–vii.

1970. "Kutchin Concepts of Reincarnation." *Western Canadian Journal of Anthropology* 2, no. 1: 67–79.

1969. "Leadership and Participation in a Kutchin Trapping Party." *Contributions to Anthropology: Band Societies*, ed. David Damas. National Museum of Canada Bulletin 228: 56–89.

1969. "Introductory Remarks: Criteria for the Identification of Bands." *Contributions to Anthropology: Band Societies*, ed. David Damas. Bulletin 228. Ottawa: National Museum of Canada: 191–96.

1966. "Indian Living ... Old Style." In *People of Light and Dark*, pp. 100–105. Ottawa: Queen's Printer.

1966. "Martha Chapman Randle, 1910–1965." *American Anthropologist* 68: 995–96.

1966. *Metis of the Mackenzie District*. Ottawa: Canadian Research Centre for Anthropology.

1964. "The Subarctic Metis as Products and Agents of Culture Contact." *Arctic Anthropology* 2, no. 2: 50–55.

1963. "'The Dawson Boys': Peel River Indians and the Klondike Gold Rush." *Polar Notes* 5: 2–12.

1963. "The Stolen Girls. *North* 10, no. 4: 34–38.

1962. *Band Organization of the Peel River Kutchin*. Bulletin 179. Ottawa: National Museum of Canada.

1960. "Eastern Kutchin Warfare." *Anthropologica* 2: 76–94.

1960. "Some Social Functions of Kutchin Anxiety." *American Anthropologist* 62, no. 1: 122–33.

1938. "Caribou Hunt." In this volume. Typescript 35 pp. with author's note and afterword dated 1993.